VIA FOLIOS 93

Here in Cerchio

Letters to an Italian Immigrant

Constance Sancetta

BORDIGHERA PRESS

Library of Congress Control Number: 2014938383.

Printed in the United States.

Published by
BORDIGHERA PRESS
John D. Calandra Italian American Institute
25 West 43rd Street, 17th Floor
New York, NY 10036

VIA FOLIOS 93
ISBN 978-1-59954-062-7

Dedication

To Mario Chiudioni, whose devotion to Italian culture and
generosity of soul survives his life.

His life was gentle, and the elements so mixed in him that Nature
might stand up and say to all the world, 'This was a man!"
—*Julius Caesar*, Act V, Scene 5

"Here in Cerchio we don't have any worldly goods, we don't have houses or fields, the harvest is very bad, things cost a good deal."

—Maria Vasquenz, June 1913

TABLE OF CONTENTS

INTRODUCTION

During the thirty years between 1880 and 1910 several million Italians, the majority of them farmers and peasants from southern Italy, left their homes in the desperate hope of finding a better life in America. Literacy rates for these people were below 50%, probably under 30% in small villages, even if "literacy" is defined by the minimal criterion "able to write one's name". Illiterate peasants did not keep diaries, and letters to emigrants from their relatives at home were usually short, consisting of personal and family news. The few scholars who visited the villages were usually interested in folkways – traditional songs and stories, superstitions, festivals – and did not make much effort to record personal histories. As a result, we have very few firsthand descriptions of the lives and conditions of these people. The information available in the U.S. consists of scattered remarks in memoirs and oral histories by immigrants, many of whom were children when they arrived. We have little insight into the subjective experience that drove millions of southern Italians to leave their homes and families for what usually turned out to be grueling labor in an alien land. They were the ancestors of hundreds of thousands of modern Americans, and we have only an abstract idea of the reality of their lives and circumstances in their native villages.

Through a fortunate concatenation of events, a collection of letters written by an Italian farmer of the time has recently become available, now archived at the Western Reserve Historical Society in Cleveland, Ohio. Between 1910 and 1913 Antonio Vasquenz, a native of the Abruzzo village of Cerchio, wrote about forty letters totaling 25,000 words to his son Angelo, an immigrant working in the coal mines of western Pennsylvania. Unlike many *contadini*, Antonio was fully literate. He was also a talented writer and intelligent man. Over a four year period he described in detail, with vivid and sometimes pungent prose, all the events and trials of his life: family illness and death, agricultural conditions, and always, always the financial burdens.

Angelo Vasquenz married Celestina Ciofani whose family was also from L'Aquila province. They lived in Republic, Pennsylvania, for the rest of their lives, dying childless in 1954 (Angelo) and 1978 (Celestina). Upon Celestina's death her younger sister, Mary Ciofani Chiudioni, found the letters among her sister's effects and preserved them at her own home near Cleveland. Mary herself died in 2005 and her son Mario Chiudioni, in turn finding the collection, generously donated them to W.R.H.S. late in 2006. A few months later the author contacted the society's curator for Italian-American History, Pamela Dorazio Dean, expressing interest in working as a part-time volunteer, and was offered the opportunity of translating the collection as her first project.

Once the project was completed it became evident that the letters represent an exceptionally detailed picture of this man's life. Moreover, during the four-year period covered by the letters the Vasquenz family experienced events common to most villagers: death of a family member, difficulties with in-laws, pressure from creditors, crop failure, even a lawsuit. Antonio and his family serve as type specimens or representative samples of the general experience. Their story is unique to themselves in its details, but it carries the overtones of the immigrants' common experience. It speaks of the lives they left behind, the lives that influenced and to some extent determined their better-documented lives in the U.S.

Antonio himself never came to America, but his sons and nephews did. During the period covered by the letters his Meogrossi nephews (on his wife's side) were living in Nottingham, Ohio, and several of his Vasquenz nephews lived in Cleveland; two of them spent the rest of their lives there. They would have been fully aware of and deeply interested in the story told in these letters, for it reflected their own family, their own experiences, and the stresses that drove them to emigrate. More generally, there were hundreds of Antonios, older men who came to America bringing their own memories and influenced by a similar past. Antonio, a literate peasant, speaks for thousands of others who have gone silent into history. We owe it to them to tell their story.

•

This book is structured to frame the particular history of the Vasquenz family within the larger context of southern Italian village life. Part I consists of six short chapters describing the physical, agricultural, social and economic setting in the early 20th century. These chapters are not intended to provide a comprehensive description of conditions, but only enough to serve as a background for the Vasquenz story. Part II provides a summary of the information available on the members of the Vasquenz family, a short summary of the story revealed in the letters, and the full text of Antonio's letters to his son with explanatory notes inserted as needed. A final chapter reproduces letters from several of Angelo's female relatives that reveal the difficulties experienced by women separated from their men for prolonged periods.

All possible avenues have been explored to locate further information on these people, but after a century of time some threads cannot be reconstructed. The Family History Library provided by The Church of Jesus Christ of Latter-Day Saints contains microfilms of the civil records of births, marriages and deaths in Cerchio only between 1810 and 1865, allowing us to identify Antonio and his siblings but not the generation of their children. Ship manifest records and other documents such as the U.S. census forms provided at web sites (including Ancestry.com and EllisIsland.org), have been used to construct a partial story for the Vasquenz and their relatives who immigrated to the U.S., but by their nature cannot provide a continuous record. There is no way to track movements of migrant workers within the United States, nor their return to Italy. On-line searches are dependent upon proper reading of orthography by those who indexed the documents. For instance, the ship manifest records for three of the Vasquenz entrants are indexed under the name "Vasquez". The tendency to repeat the same name within a family, along with occasional errors in a person's age or stated date of immigration, often make it difficult to be certain that two records refer to the same individual. We have been unable to locate descendants within the United States of any of these people, aside from Mario Chiudioni, Angelo's nephew by marriage and donor of the letters, who only met his uncle a few times when Mario himself was a child.

Mario Chiudioni was a lifelong supporter of Italian culture, and a man of great generosity. This book quite literally would not have been possible had he not donated the letters to the Western Reserve Historical Society. Pamela Dorazio Dean, curator of the Italian archives there, has been a constant friend and colleague throughout the translation of the letters and writing of this book. She and Dr. John Grabowski, Director of Research, encouraged me in this project and made several helpful suggestions as to finding a publisher. I am deeply grateful to Liliana Colage and Elda Borroni, friends who have helped to disentangle some of the complex constructions in the letters. Dr. Egidio Lunardi of Lake Erie College read an early draft of the manuscript and first urged me to contact Dr. Fred L. Gardaphe at the John D. Calendra Italian American Institute of Queens College, who took time from his own busy life to review my proposal for publication and give me his advice as to whether and where to submit it. Without his help, the book might never have come to the attention of Bordighera Press. A final tribute is due to the many contributors to web sites which have provided, in one way or another, almost all of the reference material needed to create this book, especially to the Google system for their search routines, GoogleBooks and GoogleEarth; to Wikipedia in both Italian and English versions; to Fold3 History and Genealogy Archives for scanned images and full references to microfilm publications; and to the Statue of Liberty-Ellis Island Foundation for their searchable database of ship manifests.

Translator's Notes

A ntonio Vasquenz was born in the mid-19th century and his writing preserves the formal style he learned in his youth (probably from a village priest), but also many regional and archaic features. The overall impression is that he was reasonably literate and well-educated for his time and class. His grammar and vocabulary have some regional elements, but in the main the letters are proper Italian, rather than the Abruzzo dialect which he almost certainly spoke. With the exceptions described below, his spelling is generally correct and his grammar accurate, such as correct use of the subjunctive. Appendix I provides an example of his style, transcribed directly from the letter.

Italian syntax is more flexible than English so that, for instance, the direct object may be placed at the beginning of a sentence rather than after the verb. Antonio's punctuation is minimal and somewhat random; he uses a comma for almost all breaks in the flow, and no capitalization to signal the beginning of a sentence. There are numerous cases in which he changed his mind while writing a sentence, either interjecting a remark in mid-flow or completing the sentence in a way that does not accord with the beginning. For these reasons, a literal translation of the letters would seem stilted and at times incomprehensible. I have broken up the lengthy sequences into shorter sentences with modern punctuation inserted as seems appropriate. I have also modernized some of the language, trying to stay faithful to Antonio's original style but in the form he might have used if he were writing today. In particular, Italian does not have the equivalent of contractions such as "don't" or "I'm". To use the uncontracted form would produce an effect of formality to the modern American, as would the strict translation of a verb form: "I do not understand why you have chosen to do this", versus "I don't understand why you did this." I have used contractions and simplifications like this sample on the assumption that in writing to his son Antonio would have been thinking informally. However, for the most part I have retained his somewhat rambling style in order to remain true to his character. The letters might be more comprehensible if they were heavily edited, but they would no longer be Antonio's.

It may be worth noting here some of the ways in which Antonio's grammar and spelling differ from modern Italian. In spelling, the most notable is the use of "d" for "t" in many words (*"aldro"* rather than *"altro"*) and omission of a "u" before an "o" (*"more"* instead of *"muore"*, *"poi"* instead of *"puoi"*). He often omits the letter "v" (*auto* instead of *avuto*, *riceuta* instead of *ricevuta*). A "g" is sometimes replaced by a 'c' (*"manciare"* for *"mangiare"*). An initial "h" is often omitted and an accent used instead (*ò parlato* rather than *ho parlato*). All of these cases undoubtedly reflect the way he actually spoke the words; his spelling in these cases is phonetic.

His grammar also differs, although this is less consistent. For instance, he often writes the first person past absolute as *parlò*. Today it would be *parlai*, where *parlò* is used for the third person. This can make it uncertain who took the action – the author himself or a third party. Some verbs that today take *essere* as the auxiliary are used with *avere*. He uses the regional verb *pigliare* in place of *prendere*, and the old forms *esso* and *essa* for "he" and "she".

UNCERTAINTIES AND AMBIGUITIES

Handwriting is sometimes unclear. People make mistakes when writing in a hurry (especially a scribe attempting to keep pace with a rapid speaker). If these sources of error are combined with archaic grammar and spelling, it is sometimes difficult to be certain what a given word is intended to signify. Usually one can determine it from context, but there are a few cases in which the translation represents a "reasonable guess". To provide a few examples:

1) Italian nouns, and therefore adjectives, have masculine or feminine gender, usually indicated by a terminal "-o" (masculine) or "-a" (feminine). A *contadino* is a man, a *contadina* a woman. Unfortunately, the script "a" and "o" are very similar, so that occasionally it may be difficult to be certain what noun an adjective is supposed to be modifying, and sometimes even what word is intended – *esso* and *essa* are archaic terms for "he" and "she", for instance.

2) Inability to distinguish the terminal "-a" from "-o" also can lead to occasional uncertainties in the person or tense of a verb. Italian does not normally use a pronoun for the subject, because the form of the verb in an inflected language will usually make it clear. But if the final letter is in doubt, one cannot be certain whether the word is intended to be *parlo* (I speak) or *parla* (he/she speaks). Moreover, in the case of the third person singular, the gender of the speaker is always unclear if there is no pronoun. As a final complication, the presence or absence of an accent on the terminal vowel can change not only the tense but the person of a verb – *parlo* = "I speak" while *parlò* = "he/she spoke".

A different kind of uncertainty has to do with financial and legal terms, because the words can have several meanings (tax *or* fee; rent *or* mortgage; bill of exchange *or* promissory note) and we don't know the circumstances in detail. Antonio's affairs are clearly complicated: he's borrowing from some people to pay others, his produce is sequestered, he pays a variety of taxes and fees, and there is the mortgage with Carmine d'Alessandro, for which he uses both the words for "rent" and "mortgage" in different letters. I have used the English term, which seems most likely to be correct, considering all of the letters that refer to each case.

In the few cases where we have been unable to translate a word or phrase in a meaningful way, the Italian is retained between brackets, as in [*sei decine di livori*]. This translates as "six tenths of lividity", probably not what Antonio meant to say. Italian words for which a simple translation does not exist are left in the original and defined in a footnote where they first occur.

NOTE ON WEIGHTS AND MEASURES

Antonio uses the traditional units of *coppa, salma* and *tomolo,* which may refer to either an area of land or the dry volume of produce from that area. The amounts varied widely throughout Italy. The closest analogy that I have found for Cerchio is for the town of Pescara, reported at: http://www.pe.camcom.it, a web site for the Chamber of Commerce in Pescara:

As units of land area (where 1 *ara* = 100 square meters)
1 *misura* = 1 *ara* 35 cent
1 *coppa* = 8 *are* 10 cent
1 *tomolo* = 32 *are* 42 cent

As units of dry volume:
1 *misura* = 2.33 liters
1 *coppa* = 6 *misure* = 14 liters = 0.4 bushel
1 *mezzetto* = 2 *coppe* = 28 liters = about 0.8 bushels
1 *tomolo* = 2 *mezzetti* = 56 liters = about 1.8 bushels
1 *salma* = 3 *tomoli* = 168 liters = about 5.5 bushels

Antonio uses the words in both senses and one must use context to determine which he means. For example, on June 27, 1911 he mentions a *salma* of grain which he got "from the Signora"; this would be seed grain for planting at the beginning of the season. Later in the same letter he speaks of plowing five *coppe* of fava fields, referring to the area of land.

Currency

During Antonio's youth the Abruzzo was part of the Kingdom of the Two Sicilies and the *piastra* was the basic unit of currency. After unification (1861) the Sardinian *lira* became the national currency, with 100 *centesimi* = 1 *lira*. A popular unit was the *soldo,* equal to five *centesimi* or 1/20 of a *lira*. The *soldo* was not minted after unification but the word continued to be used as a general term to mean "cash" or "money". Antonio uses the word in three senses and I have translated them as follows:

"Money" when used as a general term. Example: *Non ho soldi* = "I don't have any money."

Not translated when used as a specific amount. Example: *Le femine vogliono 30 soldi* = "The women want 30 *soldi*."

"Nickel" when used colloquially. Example: *noi stiamo senza poter comprare un soldo di fiammiferi* = "We can't buy a nickel's worth of matches."

PART I – BACKGROUND

Chapter 1
GEOGRAPHIC SETTING AND CLIMATE

The village of Cerchio (CHER-kee-o) is located in the central Apennines of Italy in L'Aquila Province of the Abruzzo region (Figures 1 and 2). The southern part of the Abruzzo, including the area of Cerchio, is also referred to as the Marsica, a name predating modern political divisions. Cerchio lies on the southern slope of Mount Sirente above the northern edge of the Fucino Plain. Distance from Cerchio to the nearest part of the plain is a little over two miles downhill. To the Bacinetto, where Antonio had some of his fields, is about three miles.

The Fucino Plain is a basin about 150 square kilometers in area, draining a region of 710 square kilometers. It is a closed basin, meaning that it has no outlet for the runoff from the surrounding mountains. Since precipitation exceeds evaporation in this region, the Fucino by nature is a large lake and has been so for most of recorded history. The deepest part of the former lake, at the eastern edge, is referred to as the Bacinetto ("little basin"). Prior to its draining it was the third-largest lake in Italy.

Mediterranean tectonics are among the most complex in the world, with elements of both compression and extension. The Apennine system as a whole is the result of compressional tectonics and uplift during the Miocene epoch related to the closing of the Mediterranean basin. In the immediate area of interest, the central Apennines are currently extending, with a series of parallel oblique faults running NW to SE. The Fucino basin is bounded on its eastern side by a series of active faults and it is the motion on these faults that accounts for the frequent earthquakes of the area.[1]

---

[1] Piccardi et al., 1999

Town records in Cerchio mention earthquakes in 1633, 1648, 1703 and 1850.[2] The latter occurred when Antonio was seven years old, and destroyed all the churches in town so that most of the town records were lost. Another devastating earthquake occurred in 1915, destroying 80% of the structures and killing 224 people.

The Mediterranean climate is monsoonal, characterized by a semiannual alternation of wind direction and moisture. In winter the winds blow from the north, bringing moisture in the form of cold rain, with snow and hail common at higher elevations such as that of Cerchio. A strong event is referred to as a *tramontana*, similar to the New England northeasterly. In summer the prevailing winds are generally from the south, producing hot and dry conditions. During a *scirocco* the southerly winds are laden with dust derived from the Sahara Desert, analogous to the southern California Santa Ana.

---

[2] http://www.cerchio.terremarsicane.it/index.php?module=CMpro&func=viewpage&pageid=20

Chapter 2
LOCAL HISTORY AND DEVELOPMENT OF THE FUCINO

BRIEF HISTORY OF THE AREA[3]

One theory holds that the name Cerchio (literally "circle") is derived from the original shape of the prehistoric settlement at this location. Today the village proudly calls itself "the roundest town in the Marsica."[4] A few Bronze Age items found during excavations indicate that a village was already present well before the Roman period. Cerchio and the neighboring villages appear sporadically in church documents from the 9th century on, Cerchio itself being first mentioned in 818 C.E.

In the mid 11th century Norman soldiers of fortune, led by Robert Guiscard established the County of Sicily, later extended to the Kingdom of Sicily in 1103 under Roger II. The Kingdom of Sicily was based in that island but incorporated the entirety of southern Italy with the Abruzzo as its northern extent. Throughout the Middle Ages and Renaissance there were continual power struggles between the kingdom and the popes in Rome, with numerous alliances and invasions involving the French and the Germans. Ultimately, the kingdom was acquired by the Spanish crown under Ferdinand II of Aragon around 1500 and, in 1759, was granted to Ferdinand IV, younger son of the Spanish king, as a separate kingdom. Ferdinand himself derived from a branch of the French Bourbon family, and the Kingdom of Naples (a.k.a. Kingdom of the Two Sicilies) is also referred to as the Bourbon kingdom.

---

[3] Most of the information in this section is derived from the History link (*storia*) at www.cerchio.terremarsicane.it; for full citation see footnote 2 above.

[4] http://cerchio.it.gg/ Motto on the home page "Il paese più tondo della Marsica"

Throughout this time Cerchio and the neighboring villages were feudatory possessions of various powerful families, including the Colonna of Rome, the Piccolomini, the Berardi, and the Peretti. Documentary history of the town consists of church records which mostly refer to religious matters such as construction and modification of the churches and donations of artistic works by wealthy individuals[5].

The records mention an outbreak of plague in 1657, and earthquakes in 1633, 1648, and 1703. The latter occurred a few years after the death of King Carlo II, during a period of war with the French and a failure of the blood of San Gennaro in Naples to liquify on the scheduled date. It is perhaps no coincidence that shortly after these disasters, in 1705, Saints John and Paul Martyr were chosen as patron saints of the town, and a church was built in their honor.

At the end of the 18th century Napoleon invaded Italy and proclaimed the Roman Republic in 1798. King Ferdinand IV of Naples called the people of the Abruzzo to arms and there were several skirmishes in which Cerchiese participated. The town history notes that there were also citizens who espoused the republican party. As always during times of unrest, brigandage increased, with demands for protection money imposed on the villages. The Bourbon army was defeated in 1799 and the king fled to Sicily. He returned to Naples after the defeat of Napoleon in 1812 and was confirmed in possession by the Congress of Vienna in 1815.

Italy was unified under Victor Emmanuel II of Sardinia in 1861 after the successful invasion of Garibaldi and his famous Thousand. The Abruzzo, along with the rest of the Kingdom of the Two Sicilies, became part of the new Kingdom of Italy, along with the Papal States, which were taken over by an army from the north later that year. Rome alone was left to the pope, and relations between the secular government and the Vatican remained poor for dec-

---

5   http://www.cerchio.terremarsicane.it/index.php?module=CMpro&func=viewpage&pageid =20

ades, with anticlerical actions by the government and papal pronouncements ordering the faithful not to conform to national requirements, such as the institution of civil marriage licenses. It was not until 1929 that an agreement was reached, with the pope surrendering all claims to secular power and Vatican City recognized as an independent polity.

Although not germane to the Vasquenz story, it should be noted that southern Italians and Sicilians were bitterly disappointed by their reduced status in the new kingdom. Many of the regional leaders had hoped for more autonomy, with Italy structured as a confederation. This, along with subversive activities supported by the exiled Francisco II of Naples, led to much disorder and brigandage throughout the south. The new kingdom, dominated by northern Italians, is often accused of showing little interest in confronting the formidable problems of southern poverty and ignorance, with the regrettable result that development in southern Italy even today is behind that of the north by almost any measure (e.g. literacy, employment, crime).

DRAINING OF LAKE FUCINO[6]

The Romans made several attempts to drain the lake, most successfully under Claudius, but with the decline of the Roman Empire the engineering works failed and the Fucino returned to its natural state. Over the centuries, Cerchio and the other villages experienced both advantages and drawbacks from the presence of the lake. On the positive side, it provided a free source of protein in the form of fish, and the large body of water moderated the local climate, permitting the cultivation of olive and fruit trees. On the other hand, malaria and other mosquito-borne diseases were a chronic problem, and in years of heavy precipitation lake levels might rise enough to flood low-lying villages and fields. Hydrologic measurements from the late 18th to the mid 19th century indicate that water depth varied from 4-20m.

---

[6] Most of the information in this section can be found in Linoli, 2005 and Felice, 2007

From 1789 on the king authorized several attempts to renovate or replace the Roman drainage system, but work rarely got beyond the stage of assessment as a result of political upheaval, lack of financing, and the rooted objections of the local fishermen and their landlords, who received a large profit from their share of the catch. In 1852 a French businessman living in Naples established an investment company to finance draining of the lake, in return for which the company would be granted ownership of the land exposed. Fifty percent of the company stock was purchased initially by the Roman banker Alessandro Torlonia, and by 1854 he had acquired the remaining stock, thus making him sole owner of the project.

Torlonia's investment was substantial, as he was determined to do the job properly. He is reputed to have said, "Either Torlonia will drain the Fucino or the Fucino will drain Torlonia." The main project took almost fifteen years and represented the most ambitious engineering possible at the time, with most of the specialists imported from France, since Italy lacked professionals at this level of skill. The project was completed in 1870, when Antonio was 27 years old. Another eight years were required for the last of the water to drain away and for secondary ditches to be installed. It is estimated that the total expense was 43 million *lire*, about ten times the original capital investment of the company. The project resulted in 210 km of roads, 100 km of canals, and 648 km of ditches.

Considerable debate continues today as to the overall costs and benefits of the draining, and more specifically the role of Torlonia. Some side effects became evident within a few years: while malaria was eliminated, the local climate was altered when the moderating effect of the water disappeared. Seasonal extremes of colder winters and hotter summers developed, with loss of olives and fruit trees. Villagers lost their livelihood as fishermen and were forced to become tenant farmers, while Torlonia and other large land-holders made immense profits. Felice provides a thorough discussion of the many elements of this controversy, describing the flaws in the system but also assessing the practical limitations for Torlonia along with his admitted lack of effort to improve matters as they degenerated.[7]

DEVELOPMENT OF FUCINO AGRICULTURE

In 1875 Victor Emmanuel II conferred upon Torlonia the title of Prince of Fucino and confirmed his ownership rights to the newly-exposed land for a 90-year period. The original intent had been to establish units of 20-25 hectares each (50-60 acres), resulting in 400-500 farms. For various financial, social and political reasons the actual result was a mixed system in which the Torlonia Administration directly managed 2,800 hectares, a very small area of 900 hectares went to sharecroppers and by far the largest (9,300 hectares) were subleased by Torlonia or by others to whom he granted concessions.[8] The subleases were repeatedly subdivided and subleased down to tenant farmers like Antonio. By the turn of the 20th century each tenant was working about one hectare (2.5 acres), and paying a rent that was multiplied several times through a sequence of sublessees.[9] Subleasing was formally forbidden in the contracts, but the prohibition was universally ignored.

Yield from the soil was initially very high since the lake sediments were rich in nutrients and organic matter, and the new Fucino was expected to be the "breadbasket of Rome". In the first year of cultivation fully 40% of the area was planted for wheat, in rotation with maize and beans. However, uncontrolled harvesting and inefficient methods led to a marked decline in production by as much as two thirds. Following the recession of the early 1880's the cultivation of beets was introduced. Initially they were used primarily for animal fodder (the animals in turn producing manure for fertilization), but following construction of a sugar mill at Avezzano an increasingly large amount went for sugar production. While cereal cultivation remained the primary area of focus, with a

---

[7] Felice, Chap. 4, Section 4, pp 180-185

[8] Felice, *ibid.* p. 181

[9] Felice, *ibid.* p. 182

highly-profitable variety of wheat developed (*grano fucense*), the consistent annual production and return on sugar beets "finally shows the beginnings of an integrated agricultural and industrial system"[10]. Cultivation of potatoes was also intensified, and the system of roads and canals expanded. Peoples' banks (Chapter 6) were established to provide loans for small farmers and a rail line was built between Avezzano and Rome.

At the turn of the 20th century the German company operating the sugar mill was granted the entire area of the Bacinetto for beet production and was renamed the Roman Sugar Company. A crisis arose in 1910 when the government proposed to raise taxes on sugar. Roman Sugar, in order to keep the price level, countered with a reduction in the price paid to farmers for the beets, leaving people like Antonio on the losing end and leading to social unrest and strikes. This may explain Antonio's letter of Jan. 1, 1911 in which he refers to Angelo's objection to his planting of beets and explains why it is still financially necessary for him to do so. Angelo may have sympathized with the strikers and wanted his father to plant something else in order to support the resistance.

By 1919, a local newpaper reported the annual product of the Fucino as 600,000 quintals of beets, 300,000 each of potatoes and hay, 200,000 of wheat and 100,000 of legumes, making beets by far the most important product.[11]

---

[10] Felice, *ibid.* p. 188

[11] Newspaper "Il Domani", July 31 and August 18, 1919. Cited by Felice, *ibid.* p. 261

Chapter 3
CONTADINI AND VILLAGE LIFE[12]

The term *contadino* ("countryman") is best translated as "agricultural worker" and comprises a range of positions. In general, anyone who derives his income from working on the land
is a *contadino*, even one who owns the land. Only when a person is
wealthy enough to become a gentleman of leisure with others per-
forming the labor does he become a *proprietario* ("landowner").

The lowest level of *contadino* corresponds to our field hand or
hired worker. These people have no financial interest in the land or
the produce, and are paid a set wage for each day of work in the
fields of others. Field workers included many women, working
sporadically as their other duties allowed. Antonio seems to have
hired mostly women for the routine work in his fields, and usually
refers to them as *giornate* ("day workers"). He uses the same term
to refer to the daily wages paid, which at one point was 30 *soldi*,
corresponding to about $6.00 per day (May 6, 1910).

A second category are sharecroppers, who work on the lands of
others for a defined share in the produce, the remainder going to
the landowner. The *contadino* is then free to sell some of the produce for cash and to retain some for his family's consumption.
Church lands belonging to monasteries and nunneries were often
worked by sharecroppers, thus providing food for the religious
with no expense or labor on their part. Arrangements between
sharecroppers and their employers varied widely in different areas.
The landowner typically received from one third to one half of the
produce and usually provided housing for the sharecropper and his

---

[12] Information in this section is derived from Villari, 1903 and King and Okey, 1913.

family, either among the fields or in a nearby village. He might also cover the cost of seed grain and major expenses such as plowing.

The last group of *contadini* are the tenant farmers, who rent one or more plots of land from the landowner at a fixed annual rate. Antonio is one of these, renting his Fucino fields from the Torlonia Administration for 310 *lire* (comparable to $1,445 today; Appendix II). Here too arrangements varied as to responsibilities; in Antonio's case he is responsible for all expenses including purchase of seed grain (which he buys on credit), hiring of day workers and paying the plowers and harvesters, who were probably part of the Torlonia apparatus. His contract probably also specified the range of crops that would be accepted and set other limits on his options.

A successful tenant farmer might rent several small plots of land or even own one or two plots outright, acquired through inheritance, marriage, or purchase. Such plots were often several miles apart, so that much time was consumed in travel from home to the fields. Antonio apparently had fields in two areas, which he refers to as "the Fucino fields" and "the land in the Bacinetto". He comments several times on the difficulty of travelling to them without a draft animal, since they would have been several miles from his home.

Most *contadini* rented their homes from their employer or a landlord in the village. Antonio, near the top of the hierarchy, apparently owned his house, which was probably in much better condition that the dirt-floored one-room hovel of the poorest people. Electrification had not reached Cerchio at the time of the letters, and there was no indoor plumbing. Water was acquired from a common well or natural spring and kept in large earthenware urns (the *conca*) outside the house. Village women did the washing in a large stone basin, usually designed to tap the spring or a small stream so that there was a continuous supply of running water.

Even the poorest *contadino* maintained a kitchen garden if there was any land associated with his house. Here the family grew vegetables such as onions, tomatoes, peppers and perhaps some beans. Many people had a few vines from which they made their own wine. There might be a few chickens, with eggs providing a source of animal protein, and more successful people might have a goat or two for cheese. Antonio mentions a kitchen garden with almond and plum trees, but apparently did not have any vines since he has to buy his wine from others. He keeps chickens, and also has a stable with either a donkey or a mare at different times.

Contadino diet was limited, but better than that of the urban poor. They had their kitchen gardens, possibly domestic animals, and herbs such as thyme, rosemary and fennel grow wild in much of southern Italy. The animals were only eaten for very special events, while eggs and cheese provided protein. A sharecropper or tenant farmer could also keep some of his produce for family consumption. Antonio conforms to this pattern, saying at one point that they have been subsisting on bread, eggs and potatoes, with wine only when it is necessary to sweeten a deal with the plowmen (Apr. 15, 1912). When recovering from his injury he had one hen and a few kilos of meat to build up his strength (May 6, 1910). When his produce is not sequestered, he also has beans available.

Prior to unification, village priests provided education to villagers, and Antonio, who was born in 1843, probably studied with the priest, explaining his surprisingly good handwriting, spelling and grammar. After unification the Vatican forbade priests to teach even basic literacy, leading to several generations of illiterate villagers. Antonio sent his sons to some friends to give them some basic training (February 26, 1916), but their handwriting, spelling and grammar are notably worse than his.[13]

The vast majority of *contadini* were Catholics, although their version of the faith was light on theology and focussed on worship of the Madonna and saints, religious festivals, and a strong dose of superstition. Even today, women tend to be more devout and to attend church more regularly than the men. When the papal lands

---

[13] Letters from brother Tommaso and some draft documents by Angelo are included in the collection at W.R.H.S.

were absorbed into the kingdom after unification the popes retreated into the Vatican whence they railed against the "atheistic" regime. The higher clergy supported the pope, preaching and writing numerous works against the secular government. These controversies meant little to villagers, and the effect was to separate the church hierarchy from the lives of most people, who continued to follow their own version of religion. While they might consult the local priest on spiritual matters, they paid little attention to papal policy.

Antonio provides a typical example of this attitude: he refers to God piously in many letters, and twice mentions recourse to the Virgin: when he goes to the Madonna della Libera to give thanks for his recovery (spring 1910) and when he advises his newly-married son to rely on the Madonna as his protectress (May 8, 1913). For illness such as his wife's edema or an outbreak of cholera he trusts in Saint Rocco, a medieval saint credited with curing people of plague. During the cholera epidemic Pius X reduced the number of public festivals with the praiseworthy motive of limiting contagion. Antonio is disgusted with this decree, saying that the pope is practically a protestant. From the tone of his letter, it seems that what he most resented was losing the holiday from work, rather than any spiritual deprivation (Sept. 27, 1911).

Southern Italians have preserved a series of rituals concerned with death, many of which persisted well into the 20th century. The deceased is laid out in the home for several days, during which a watch is kept by friends and neighbors with continuous prayers. Crepe ribbons or wreathes are mounted on the door and left until they disintegrate from weathering. After this period (usually three days) the body in its coffin is taken to the church for a mass, and then to the village graveyard. November 1st and 2nd span the Day of the Dead; on the 1st gifts of food are taken to the cemetery and the dead, in turn, bring gifts of toys and candy to the children of each house on November 2nd. Antonio provides a moving description of the death and funeral of his daughter Pasquccia (Mar. 17, 1911 and May 10, 1911) in which he refers to the *riuscita* (literally "coming out again"), apparently a local term for the procession from the home to the mass.

Chapter 4
AGRICULTURAL MATTERS

Agricultural techniques varied widely in Italy during the time of interest. Many *contadini* were still using hand tools, but the Fucino system was one of the most advanced for its time, being in effect an early form of agribusness. Antonio was just twenty when the draining was complete and may well have been one of the first group of tenant farmers enrolled. Apparently he leased his fields directly from the Torlonia Administration, preserving him from some of the ills of repeated subdivision and subleasing, although there may still have been significant changes in his contract over the decades. His rent to the Torlonia Administration (310 *lire*) is even higher than that quoted by Felice for a subleased hectare in the Bacinetto (280 *lire*),[14] although it is possible that he worked more than one hectare.

Machinery such as plows, threshers, and combine harvesters were probably owned by the Torlonia Administration and Antonio's contract almost certainly required him to use their services, although he may have been allowed to negotiate a rate. He refers several times to his need to pay the plowers and reapers, saying that the Colonica family wanted 20 *lire* for plowing (May 1910) and that he had to pay from five to nine and a half *lire* per person per day (115 *lire* total) as the cost of reaping (August 15, 1910). Through most of the decades of his life this equipment would have been drawn by teams of horses. At the time of the letters the internal combustion engine was just being developed for farm machinery, but it seems likely that the horse-drawn system was still the one used.

---

[14] Felice, *ibid.* p. 181

The harvested crops were delivered to a central warehouse, where they would have been weighed and assessed. Antonio received whatever price was currently set for each kind of produce after any debts and fees were deducted. He does not give any details on these matters, so we have only Felice's comments that contracts could be highly restrictive[15]. The warehouse managers then distributed the produce to the appropriate customers. When his products were not sequestered, he could take home a portion for family consumption. He may also have been able to reserve some of the maize or wheat as seed stock for the next year, although usually he has to buy them from others.

We can infer from the letters that Antonio rented fields in two areas. He usually speaks of the Bacinetto fields, where he grows the root crops, maize, *cordeschi* and beans. "The Fucino fields" must have been elsewhere in the plain, and seem to have been where he planted grain and hay. Probably his Fucino fields were within a larger area of holdings all planted in grain, so that sowing and reaping could be done efficiently over a single large area.

Apparently he could choose which crops to plant in the Bacinetto, since he debates with Angelo about the merits of planting beets in 1911. In practice he seems to have planted some of each, although the letters are spotty enough that there may have been some crop rotation. It is possible that certain minimum requirements were set, e.g. for wheat, which was intended to be one of the primary products of the "Roman breadbasket."[16] In various letters he mentions wheat, beets, maize, potatoes, various beans, hay, and the unidentified *cordeschi* (presumably a dialect term). All of these, aside from the *cordeschi*, are mentioned by Felice as being the primary crops for the Fucino system.

The beets, as noted above (Chapter 2) were grown for sugar and would have been delivered to the processing plant at Avezzano, probably by the warehouse staff. Most likely his potatoes were

---

[15] Felice, *ibid.* p. 184

[16] Felice, *ibid.* p. 179

the *Patate degli Altiplani d'Abruzzo*, a variety developed for the Abruzzo region and mostly used for potato flour[17]. The family does eat the potatoes when at their lowest ebb, but Antonio doesn't like them much and at one point calls them "those miserable potatoes", possibly because the variety has a mealy texture and little flavor. The maize, usually called *granturco* in Italian but referred to by Antonio with the dialect term *mazzocche*, was probably used for animal feed as it is still in Europe today.

Root crops, legumes and maize had a single cultivation cycle, being planted in late winter to early spring and harvested in the fall. Wheat, as elsewhere in the northern hemisphere, had two seasonal forms. Hard (winter) wheat was planted in the late fall and sprouted before the winter freeze. It remained dormant until early spring when growth resumed, and was harvested after ripening in April or early May. The hardest wheat in Italy (durum) is mostly used for making pasta. Soft wheat is planted in the spring and harvested in late summer. It is primarily used for bread and other baked goods.

Grain accounts for most of Antonio's agricultural expenses. Like farmers elsewhere, he buys seed on credit at the beginning of each planting season, hoping to sell enough from the harvest to repay the loans – a hope in which he is rarely successful, being forced to postpone the creditors for a year or more. Plowmen must be hired to break the soil, day workers to remove the worst of the weeds during the growing season, and then again to assist in the harvest. Wheat has a short window of peak ripeness when it must be harvested and the whole procedure from reaping to storage must be completed before a rainstorm creates conditions for rot. For this reason, harvest is a labor-intensive activity, with workers in the fields from dawn to dusk. Antonio belongs to a *camparole*, a sort of farming collective consisting of a group of farmers and field hands who harvest several fields in turn.

---

[17] Italian Wikipedia entry under "Patata degli Altipiani d'Abruzzo", last accessed 2/17/2012

In the first few decades of the Fucino system, crop rotation was used to regenerate the soil. During the improvements of the late 1880's, animal husbandry was expanded; cattle, sheep and pigs were fed on the side products of the plants (e.g. leaves and stems of the root crops and beans), and their manure used to enrich the soil.[18] Antonio refers to nitrate at one point (August 15, 1912), so artificial fertilizers may have become available by then. He makes almost no reference to forage animals, and so we cannot tell whether he actually owned any himself. One letter (February 26, 1911) makes a passing reference to "vaccine in the Fucino" and in another (Sept. 27, 1912) he mentions having promised the side products to "the man who came for the sowing", saying that otherwise he would have "sold the maize left on the ground to get food for the animals". This suggests that he did support animals in some way, but it is possible that he was not the owner but simply contributing to a group expense.

Abruzzo farmers, like those elsewhere, face the constant possibility of crop loss from severe weather events. A *tramontata* bringing strong hail can destroy the wheat at any time of year. Antonio expresses frequent concern for the crops during both spring and summer *tramontana* events; in July 1911 he remarks that a severe thunderstorm has destroyed the crops in fields to the south and everyone is hurrying to get the reaping done. Equally serious was summer drought, affecting all crops. Antonio's crops are damaged by drought in the summers of 1912 and 1913.

Anyone who has traveled in rural Italy has seen the poppies and vetch flowering in the fields, lending a charm to the passing scene. The charm does not extend to the farmer, who wages a constant battle against such weeds. Antonio complains frequently about poppies, vetch, and also alfalfa, remarking that days of work won't be enough to clear them and that they can only be removed after the harvest by winnowing and sieving. Italian has a specific

---

[18] Felice, *ibid.* p. 185-6.

verb for this procedure: *svecchiare* (literally, "to de-vetchify") meaning to separate the inedible material from the grain.

Finally, there are insect pests and fungal diseases. Antonio says at one point that the beans have *polci* (tentatively translated as "aphids") and in June 1913 a wet spell was followed by rust, a fungal disease of grain, which gives a reddish color to the infected parts.

Chapter 5
POLITICAL AND LEGAL SYSTEMS

Italy was a constitutional monarchy from unification until the end of World War II, with government and legal systems derived from those of France, a relict of the Napoleonic Republic. The legislature was bicameral, with the Senate (upper house) appointed for life by the king and consisting of people from the upper classes such as those of high military rank, diplomats, former Deputies, and judges. The lower house, the Chamber of Deputies, consisted of elected representatives from each geographic constituency. During the period covered by the letters, the franchise was open to all literate adults over 21 who paid certain minima in tax or rents. Villari states the minimum land rent as £20 English sterling in the early 20th century.[19] This works out to about 500 *lire* in 1910 (Appendix II) and probably disqualified Antonio from voting, if his annual rent was indeed 310 *lire* (March 17, 1912). The literacy and financial requirements together meant that only about 7% of the population was eligible to vote.[20] The deputies frequently served as *padrone* to their constituents, just as American legislators do today, doing various favors and helping them with problems. When Antonio wants to transfer his lease on the Fucino fields to his wife, the local deputy makes the arrangements for him with the Torlonia Administration in Rome, and also provides a loan to Antonio's wife to tide them over during his illness (June 7, 1910).

At the other end of the scale, each *comune* (town or village) had an elected mayor and town council, with broader limits of franchise. These dealt with everyday matters such as village infrastruc-

---

[19] Villari, p. 128

[20] Villari, loc. cit. p. 128

ture and schools. Between the local and national levels was a complex bureaucracy of prefects, subprefects, and councilors for each province and district, all of them employees of the state. Overlapping jurisdictions led to a total of eight different entities with some authority over a given town, leading to massive inefficiency and delays.

The Italian legal system is patterned on that of France and has several features unfamiliar to Americans, the most striking being that there is no jury at the lower levels; verdict as well as sentence is rendered by the judge. The judge also poses all questions to the witnesses, so that there is no direct cross-examination. Lawyers for prosecution and defense argue their case to the judge and suggest questions to be asked of the witnesses, but the questioning is at the judge's discretion.

Italians are notorious for their litigious nature, filing lawsuits as a way to settle all personal differences and also immediately appealing any decision that goes against them. Well into the 20th century, lawyers enjoyed the opportunity to display their rhetorical skills, and since they were paid by their clients for each day in court they had no incentive to expedite matters. The judge similarly lacked incentive, with the result that the courts were clogged by the mass of backlogged cases. Antonio provides a perfect example: In summer 1911 his produce is sequestered by several creditors and he files a *reclamo*, a protest and request for reconsideration, in his wife's name (August 17, 1911). Convinced of his position, he refuses to settle out of court unless the creditors repay him for the court costs he has already encountered, waive all interest payments, and agree to accept only partial payment of the debts for a while (September 4, 1911). Not surprisingly, they decline and Antonio sinks into the morass of the court at Celano. The case is postponed nine times over one and a half years; sometimes the judge cancels the session without hearing a single case. Aside from the initial fee to file the *reclamo*, Antonio must pay a fee each time the case is put on the docket, a fee to subpoena the witnesses, and "gifts" to the lawyer and the witnesses. But the longer he waits and the more he has invested, the more determined he becomes to hold out in order to recoup his expenses, even though throughout this time he has no access to his produce sequestered in the warehouse – a true case of cutting off one's nose to spite the face. The case gets part way through trial by spring 1913, but at this point the judge wants to see a copy of the original distraint order, and the letters end before we learn the final result.

Chapter 6
ECONOMIC MATTERS AND FINANCIAL PROBLEMS
OF THE *CONTADINI*

After unification the newly-formed nation found itself with limited resources and extensive financial demands. Especially in the former Kingdom of Naples, infrastructure such as roads and bridges was minimal and public schools nonexistent, it having been the policy of the ruling classes to keep the peasants as isolated and passive as possible. Agricultural methods and industry were generally far behind those of northern Europe and the United States. Any attempt to extract funds from the wealthy landlords would have been met with fierce resistance, possibly leading to revolution. The government was therefore forced to borrow large amounts, resulting in a massive national debt, and taxes of various sorts became the only feasible source of money. Most of these taxes were similar to those paid by Americans today, although we do not always think of them as such.

Taxes and imposts at the national level included an income tax, property tax, sales tax, and import duties, all at high rates. The land tax, for instance, was typically at least 20% of assessed value and sometimes twice that.[21] Any improvement of the land would therefore raise the value and result in increased taxes, with the result that landowners usually made no effort to improve their fields. Income tax, ranging from 7-20%, was assessed on gross income rather than net, so that even if an individual's expenses outweighed his income the tax was still imposed.[22] Incomes below 500 *lire* were

---

[21] Villari, *ibid.* p. 48-49

[22] Villari, *ibid.* p. 49; King and Okey, *ibid.* p. 139

exempt from tax. Antonio does not mention an income tax specifically, so he may have been below this limit.

In addition, there were also taxes levied by the *comune*, including a sort of import duty on food and drink brought into the town (the *octroi*), a property tax, and the arbitrarily-assessed "family tax." For the latter, a village official would examine the house and moveable goods and make an estimate of their value, with a corresponding tax assigned. Antonio mentions an annual tax paid to the town of 30 *lire*, which might be either a property tax on his house or the family tax. In addition, certain items such as a horse or mule were taxed specifically, like the property tax charged by some American states on automobiles. Sales tax on basic items like food and drink was compounded of national and communal taxes. All in all, as much as 30% of a person's income might disappear in taxes.[23]

Finally, there were numerous taxes or fees associated with various procedures. For instance, when Antonio and Angelo signed a mortgage contract they had to pay a fee to the notary for preparing the document, a fee for the document itself, and yet another fee to have it officially registered. If Antonio wants a copy for his own use, that is a further fee of six to seven *lire*. As mentioned above, he paid a fee for the initial filing of his *reclamo*, and a fee each day the case appeared on the docket, even if the judge never got around to hearing it. (See Appendix II for a list of Antonio's expenses and their comparable cost in modern U.S. dollars.) Several of the letters contain examples in which Antonio tries to argue with the notary that the cost of a copy should be included with the original fee for preparation; the reply invariably was No.

Taxes and fees were far from the only financial commitments of a farmer. Antonio's letters repeatedly speak of the loans he has received for seeds, each of which accrued interest. In other cases he gives the amount he owes to a person but does not tell us the purpose of the original loan. For all of these loans he signed an IOU, which would also have incurred the notary and filing fees men-

---

[23] Villari, *ibid.*, footnote on p. 48; King and Okey, p. 138

tioned above. Often he persuaded his creditors to accept only the interest for one year, promising to pay the principal later. This, of course, meant that his total payment was much higher, since interest would have compounded from year to year. In a few cases he gives numbers which show that his interest on loans was as high as 20%. Then there were the daily wages to field workers, and seasonal expenses for plowing and harvest described above (Chapter 4).

Antonio's annual rent to the Torlonia Administration for the fields was 310 *lire* (equivalent to $1,455 today). The local administrator apparently allowed him some leeway, but there came a point when he was compelled to pay at least that minimum or risk losing the lease. This fear was ever-present in his mind; numerous letters implore Angelo to send more money "or we may lose the fields". He shows an interesting attitude toward the fields, mentioned by Felice as a common one in the Fucino area,[24] in which tenants thought of their leases as real property to be bought and sold or transferred to others. He originally promised "the Fucino fields" as a dowry for his daughter Pasquala, although he later reneged on the promise, arguing that it would leave him with nothing to live on. In spring 1910 when he is in danger of death he transfers these fields to his wife (with the approval of the Torlonia representative), and later he and his wife write a will leaving the fields to Angelo and Agostino, though at one point he comments that "the government won't allow it".

Finally, there is the confusing matter of Angelo's mortgage with Carmine d'Alessandro. The letters are not consistent on this topic, but the main story seems to be that Angelo had bought a house in town (and possibly also a stable) on a mortgage co-signed with his father. Letters in 1910 and 1911 mention the debt Angelo owes to the notary for preparing and registering the mortgage document (75 *lire*), plus a further amount for a tax payment, which the notary apparently made on his behalf. When they finally pay off the mortgage in November 1912, Antonio provides an itemized list that in-

---

[24] Felice, p. 184-185.

cludes the principal (400 *lire*), recording and document fees (113 *lire* plus 30 *lire*), and a refund for property taxes paid by d'Alessandro (originally 70 *lire*, but a compromise was reached for 66 *lire*). The net result, to Antonio's rage, is that the incidental expenses add up to a full 50% of the original loan.

Large national banks did not have branches in small villages at this time, but there were several other entities that provided services such as savings accounts and small loans. The post office in Italy, as elsewhere in Europe, provides passbook savings accounts which serve as a primary place for people to deposit their funds. Antonio several times mentions his own account, where he deposits any profit he makes from sale of his produce. There were also people's banks, rather like a credit union, in which individuals could buy shares. People's banks made small loans to farmers and businessmen to buy supplies and equipment at low rates of interest. Share-owners then received dividends derived from the interest payments. In 1910 Antonio mentions the need to repay 200 *lire* to a bank, from which he later gets another 100-*lire* loan – very likely one of the people's banks.

PART II – THE VASQUENZ STORY

Chapter 7
THE VASQUENZ FAMILY AND FRIENDS

The name Vasquenz appears to be of Spanish origin. The first Vasquenz may have been a Spanish official assigned to the village by the Bourbon court, perhaps as a notary or even governor of the town. The family must have valued literacy, given Antonio's well-formed script, good spelling and grammar, and his knowledge of punctuation and arithmetic. There were no public schools when he was a child, so he probably studied with the local priest. The name Vasquenz seems to have been been unique to Cerchio; ship manifest records between 1900 and 1915 reveal about fifteen men named Vasquenz entering through the port of New York and all of them were from Cerchio.[25] Aside from the three sons of Antonio described below, several of these immigrants can be identified with certainty as their first cousins who were living in Cleveland during the time period covered here. The documentary record available on-line is fragmentary, since Italian names are frequently misspelled by American compilers of databases, and Italian databases are not on-line.

The family of immediate interest (Figure 3) is that of Antonio Vasquenz, who was born in Cerchio on December 5, 1843,[26] when Abruzzo was still part of the Kingdom of Naples and the Fucino was a large lake. Village population at the time was around 1,300 people.[27] Antonio was in his late teens when Italy was unified, and

---

[25] *Passenger and Crew Lists of Vessels Arriving at New York, 1897-1957* (National Archives Microfilm Publication T715); Records of the Immigration and Naturalization Service, Record Group 85. Scanned images were accessed through http://www.ellisisland.org, using a variety of spellings for the last name.

[26] Family History Library of the Church of Jesus Christ of Latter-Day Saints, *Registri dello stato civile di Cerchio (L'Aquila), 1809-1865* , Microfilm #1174378, Item 11: Nati 1843, entry #36.

[27] http://www.cerchio.terremarsicane.it/index.php?module=CMpro&func=viewpage& pageid=20

about thirty when draining of Fucino lake was fully completed. He may have been one of the villagers to receive shares in the fields during the first distribution. By 1910, when the letters commence, he was a tenant farmer leasing his fields from the Torlonia Administration. Antonio's story is told in his own words below. He lived until at least early 1916, when he would have been 73 years old.

Antonio married Maria Domenica Meogrossi fu Salvatore.[28] By 1910 they had three adult sons and two daughters, both married with one daughter each. The oldest son, Tommaso was born in late 1878 or early 1879,[29] and is a rather shadowy figure. He married Maria Rosalia Mione (Rosa)[30] some time prior to 1906 when he emigrated to America, entering New York on January 14, 1906 going to join his brother Angelo in Uniontown, PA.[31] He seems to have moved around in Pennsylvania, unable to find a satisfactory job. His wife Rosa joined him at the end of 1909 in Mount Carmel, PA[32], but by March of 1910 they were in Wilburton, PA, where Tommaso describes himself as "already out of work" in a letter to his newly-arrived brother.[33] In June 1913 they were in Martin, PA,[34] and thereafter they disappear from the documentary record.

---

[28] Antonio's letter of July 11, 1911.

[29] Based on his age at immigration.

[30] Her maiden name is shown on the ship manifest when she entered the U.S.

[31] Tommaso Vasquenz, *S.S. Italia* Passenger Manifest, January 14, 1906; list 3 (large stamp, upper right) p. 134 (small stamp on right), line 10 *Passenger and Crew Lists of Vessels Arriving at New York, 1897-1957* (National Archives Microfilm Publication T715, roll 657); Records of the Immigration and Naturalization Service, Record Group 85. Accessed through http://www.ellisisland.org

[32] Ma. Rosalia Mione, *S.S. Cedric* Passenger Manifest, December 31, 1909; list 9 (large stamp, upper right) p. 148 (small stamp on right), line 17. *Passenger and Crew Lists of Vessels Arriving at New York, 1897-1957* (National Archives Microfilm Publication T715, roll 1395); Records of the Immigration and Naturalization Service, Record Group 85. Accessed through http://www.ellisisland.org

[33] Letter to Angelo from Tommaso, March 3, 1910, W.R.H.S. collection

[34] Letter to Angelo from Tommaso, June 13, 1913, W.R.H.S. collection

It is very likely that they returned to Italy during World War I, as did so many others.

Antonio's second son was Angelo Fausto, born November 2, 1879[35], less than one year after Tommaso, assuming that the ages on the ship manifest records are correct. Angelo was the recipient of the letters now archived at the Western Reserve Historical Society. He first emigrated in March 1903, going to Cumberland, MD to join a cousin.[36] He probably spent most of the next six years in Pennsylvania.[37] By May 1909 he was in New York City, where his two brothers-in-law joined him.[38] He may have been on his way home at this point, because he was back in Cerchio by early 1910. He probably intended to settle down there, but after his father was seriously injured in an accident he returned to the U.S., arriving at New York on March 21, 1910 and going to join his brother Tommaso in Mount Carmel, PA.[39] He soon moved to Republic, PA, where he remained for the rest of his life, working as a coal miner. In April 1913 he married Celestina Ciofani, a young woman seventeen years his junior, whose parents were from nearby Avezzano

[35] Angelo Vasquenz, serial # U1567, *World War II Draft Cards (Fourth Registration) for the State of Pennsylvania* (National Archives Microfilm Publication M1951, Roll 326). Records of the Selective Service System, 1940 – Record Group 147. Accessed through Fold3.com.

[36] Fausto Vasquenz [sic], *S.S. Neckar* Passenger Manifest, March 27, 1903; list EEEE8 (large stamp, upper right), p. 24 (small stamp, upper right), line 23. *Passenger and Crew Lists of Vessels Arriving at New York, 1897-1957* (National Archives Microfilm Publication T715, roll 332); Records of the Immigration and Naturalization Service, Record Group 85. Accessed through http://www.ellisisland.org

[37] Ship manifest record on his return in spring 1910 indicates that 1903-1909 were spent in Pennsylvania.

[38] Indicated on the ship manifest for their immigrations, see below.

[39] Fausto Vasquez [sic] *S.S. Cedric*, Passenger Manifest, March 21, 1910; list 42 (large stamp upper right), p. 122 (small stamp, upper right), line 11. *Passenger and Crew Lists of Vessels Arriving at New York, 1897-1957* (National Archives Microfilm Publication T715, roll 1442); Records of the Immigration and Naturalization Service, Record Group 85. Accessed through http://www.ellisisland.org

and who had immigrated with her mother and siblings in 1909[40]. They had no children, and lived a modest existence in Republic. By 1930 Angelo had bought a house[41] where they lived until Angelo's death in 1954.[42] Celestina died in 1978[43] and is buried with Angelo in Lafayette Memorial Park.[44]

The third son and possibly the youngest child was Augusto (Agostino), born around 1891.[45] He emigrated for a while, joining his brother Angelo in January 1906, travelling with his brother Tommaso.[46] By 1910 he was back in Italy, imprisoned for unknown reasons at Viterbo, and apparently had gotten married to a woman named Fusara.[47] We know nothing more of Agostino. A letter from Antonio in 1916 indicates that one of the brothers had died, either a returned Tommaso or Agostino.

---

[40] Celestina Ciofani, *S.S. Europa* Passenger Manifest, February 1, 1909; list 22 (large stamp upper right), p. 46 (small stamp upper right), line 3. *Passenger and Crew Lists of Vessels Arriving at New York, 1897-1957* (National Archives Microfilm Publication T715, roll 1193); Records of the Immigration and Naturalization Service, Record Group 85. Accessed through http://www.ellisisland.org

[41] Angelo and Celesta Vasguesy [sic], Sheet 38A, lines 18 and 19, Enumeration District 26-77, Republic, Fayette County, Pennsylvania; Pennsylvaian Census of Population; *Fifteenth Census of the United States, 1930* (National Archives Microfilm Publication T626, roll 2041); Records of the Bureau of the Census, Record Group 29. Accessed through Ancestry.com.

[42] Personal communication, Mario Chiudioni, 2009

[43] Celestina Vasquenz, birth date May 25, 1896; death November 1978. Index shows place of residence as Cuyahoga County, Ohio; she died in Pennsylvania but her sister filed the report in Cuyahoga County (Mario Chiudioni, personal communication). *United States Social Security Death Index*, U.S. Social Security Administration, Death Master File. Accessed February 20, 2012 through FamilySearch (https://www.familysearch.org).

[44] Personal communication, Mario Chiudioni, 2009

[45] Based on age at immigration.

[46] Augusto Vasquenz, *S.S. Italia* Passenger Manifest, January 14, 1906; list 2 (large stamp, upper right) p. 135 (small stamp on right), line 27 *Passenger and Crew Lists of Vessels Arriving at New York, 1897-1957* (National Archives Microfilm Publication T715, roll 657); Records of the Immigration and Naturalization Service, Record Group 85. Accessed through http://www.ellisisland.org

[47] Based on comments in various letters from Antonio.

A daughter, probably christened Pasquala but always referred to by the unusual diminutive Pasquccia, married Giovanni Chichiarelli, with whom she had a daughter Marietta. Giovanni returned to the U.S. in May 1909, going to New York, where he was joining Angelo[48]. Spring of 1910 finds him in Republic, PA, along with Angelo and other relatives. At some point Pasquccia developed infectious hepatitis and lingered for more than a year. When Giovanni finally learned of the seriousness of her illness, he returned to Cerchio impetuously in September 1910. Pasquccia died on March 10, 1911, and motherless little Marietta was sent to live with the nuns in the nearby town of Aielli. Giovanni subsequently took up with another woman and very likely remarried.

The second daughter, Maria (Mariuccia) married Vincenzo di Domenico, with whom she had a daughter Antonetta. Vincenzo emigrated with Giovanni Chichiarelli in May 1909[49] and by spring 1910 was also in Republic, PA, where he stayed for several years, living and working with his brother-in-law Angelo. Vincenzo returned to Cerchio during World War I; the last we know of them is that he was serving as a soldier in 1916 and Mariuccia was in financial distress. Antonetta seems to have been a sickly child; in spring 1910 she had "problems with her eyes" (possibly trachoma) and a year later she is described as very ill (Feb. 26, 1911). She is not mentioned after that date and may have died shortly thereafter. It is perhaps significant that Antonio's letters of May 1913 mention only one niece for Angelo: Marietta, the daughter of Pasquccia.

---

[48] Giovanni Chicchiarelli [sic], S.S. *Re d'Italia* Passenger manifest, May 20, 1909; list 111 (large stamp, upper right), p. 38 (small stamp upper right), line 27. *Passenger and Crew Lists of Vessels Arriving at New York, 1897-1957* (National Archives Microfilm Publication T715, roll 1270); Records of the Immigration and Naturalization Service, Record Group 85. Accessed through http://www.ellisisland.org

[49] Vincenzo DiDomenico, S.S. *Re d'Italia* Passenger manifest, May 20, 1909; list 111 (large stamp, upper right), p. 38 (small stamp upper right), line 25. *Passenger and Crew Lists of Vessels Arriving at New York, 1897-1957* (National Archives Microfilm Publication T715, roll 1270); Records of the Immigration and Naturalization Service, Record Group 85. Accessed through http://www.ellisisland.org

Other relatives mentioned in the letters or identified through web searches include: Antonio's brothers, Isidoro and Carmine Vasquenz. Given the incompleteness of records available and potential for errors therein, coupled with the tradition of repeating names within an extended family, it is difficult to trace these people with certainty. Carmine was a few years younger than Antonio, born Aug. 16, 1846.[50] There is no evidence that he ever came to the U.S. He is probably Angelo's Uncle Carmine mentioned in several letters as co-signing various documents with Antonio. Indirect evidence from ship manifests indicates that he had several sons who were in Cleveland, Ohio, between 1909 and 1912, including Enrico.[51]

Antonio also mentions a brother Isidoro in the same letter as his nephew Enrico (May 6, 1910). This is probably the Isidoro Vasquenz who emigrated to Cleveland, arriving in N.Y. on April 24, 1909 at the age of 46, widowed, to join his nephew Enrico.[52] Isidoro died in Cleveland in 1928,[53] apparently leaving only married daughters in Cerchio.

Marietta Vasquenz was a cousin of Angelo's who was deeply in love with him. Her sad story is told in Chapter 10 below.

---

[50] Family History Library of the Church of Jesus Christ of Latter-Day Saints, *Registri dello stato civile di Cerchio (L'Aquila), 1809-1865* ; Microfilm #1174378, Item 30: Nati 1846, entry #33.

[51] No documents have been found for Enrico himself, but ship manifests for two of his brothers and his uncle all indicate that he was in Cleveland, Ohio, between 1909 and 1912.

[52] Isidoro Vasquanz [sic], *S.S. Finland* Passeger Manifest, April 24, 1909; list 14 (large stamp upper right), p. 58 (small stamp upper right), line 28, *Passenger and Crew Lists of Vessels Arriving at New York, 1897-1957* (National Archives Microfilm Publication T715, roll 1251); Records of the Immigration and Naturalization Service, Record Group 85. Accessed through http://www.ellisisland.org

[53] Ohio Department of Health, Certificates of Death 1908-1953. Index and image at *FamilySearch* (https://www.familysearch.org; last accessed February 20, 2012). Entry for Isadore Vasquenz [sic], death date September 13, 1928, Cleveland, Cuyahoga County; certificate 53714; film #1991495, image 336.

Clarice Vasquenz, another cousin, loaned Angelo money when he emigrated in 1910. He took his time about paying it back and it was not until her husband, who was in Cleveland at the time of the loan[54] came back and "yelled at her" that she demanded repayment.[55]

A letter dated Jan. 29, 1913 also mentions Luigi and Ciccantonio Vasquenz who were in worse financial straits than Antonio. Their relationship to Antonio's family cannot be determined with certainty, but a Francesco Antonio Vasquenz born in 1882 immigrated to the U.S., arriving first in 1909, at which time he was unmarried and gave his father Pietro as his closest relative in Italy[56]. In 1923 this man returned, initially to Auburn, NY and then to Cleveland, Ohio, where he became a U.S. citizen in 1929[57] and died in 1952.[58] His son Pietro was born in Italy[59] but died in

---

[54] Giovanni Battista Cipriani was in Cleveland between 1906 and 1911. He went back to Italy temporarily, and re-entered the U.S. on May 15, 1912, citing Clarice Vasquenz as his wife in Cerchio and indicating the duration of his previous time in Cleveland. *S.S. Berlin* Passenger Manifest, May 15, 1912, list 20 (large stamp, upper right), page 93 (small stamp, upper right), line 3. *Passenger and Crew Lists of Vessels Arriving at New York, 1897-1957* (National Archives Microfilm Publication T715, roll 1862); Records of the Immigration and Naturalization Service, Record Group 85. Accessed through http://www.ellisisland.org

[55] An undated note from Clarice in the Vasquenz collection at W.R.H.S. reminds him of the debt, noting that when her husband learned of it he yelled at her (*mi a gridato*). This must have been during his temporary return to Italy.

[56] Francesco Antonio Vasquenze [sic], *S.S. Königin Luise* Passenger manifest, April 30, 1909, list 33 (large stamp upper right), page 196 (small stamp upper right), line 27. *Passenger and Crew Lists of Vessels Arriving at New York, 1897-1957* (National Archives Microfilm Publication T715, roll 1255); Records of the Immigration and Naturalization Service, Record Group 85. Accessed through http://www.ellisisland.org

[57] Francesco Antonio Vasquenz, Petition for Naturalization, 1929, *Naturalization Petition and Record Books for the U.S. District Court for the Northern District of Ohio, Eastern Division, Cleveland, 1907-1946*. (National Archives Microfilm Publication M1995, roll 112) Record group 21.

[58] Frank Vasquenz, obituary in *Cleveland Press*, Feb. 5, 1952, Cleveland Necrology File, Reel #163.

[59] Shown on Francesco's Petition for Naturalization, note 56 above.

Cleveland in 1931 at the age of seven.[60] Antonio's own father was a Francesco and his grandfather a Pietro, so if this family were following the traditional alternation of names between two generations, the Cleveland Francesco Antonio may have been Antonio's nephew through a brother Pietro.

Davide and Giovanni Meogrossi, cousins of Angelo through his mother, are mentioned in a letter dated Feb 5, 1912. The collection at W.R.H.S. includes a letter from Davide dated Apr. 10, 1913 indicating that they were in Nottingham, OH at the time. The name Meogrossi is sufficiently common that the various persons found in online records cannot be identified with certainty.

Grazia Mione was probably the mother of Tommaso's wife Rosa. Grazia appears as a supportive friend of the family who gives them food in times of desperation and, being literate, transcribes family letters to be sent to the men in America.

Vincenzo Pantano, a cousin of Angelo's, was also working in Republic, PA. Vincenzo's wife and children eventually joined him, as recounted in Chapter 10.

Davide Ciaglia, Pietro and Carmine d'Alessandro, Francesco Perille *et alia* were Antonio and Angelo's creditors. Angelo contracted some debts on his own, but his father cosigned for some of them and Angelo also sent money to cover his father's expenses as well as paying off his own debts. The letters describe in detail how much money was owed to each and when they were repaid. All debts seem to have been formally arranged with IOUs signed and witnessed by a notary.

---

[60] Ohio Department of Health, Certificates of Death 1908-1953. Index and data at *FamilySearch* (https://www.familysearch.org; last accessed February 21, 2012). Entry for Peter Vasquenz, death date September 27, 1931, Cleveland, Cuyahoga County; film #1992473, image 1887.

Chapter 8
OVERVIEW OF THE STORY DERIVED FROM THE LETTERS

The Vasquenz family may have been fairly prosperous at one time, but at the time the letters begin (spring 1910) the family has fallen on hard times. Antonio was deeply in debt for loans of money to buy seed grain, to pay field workers, and to cover numerous taxes and fees. His son Angelo apparently incurred his own debts, including a mortgage on a house in town, when he returned in late 1909, probably with the intention of settling down and buying some land of his own. But matters were taken out of his hands when Antonio was badly injured in a "fall" in early February. The nature of the accident is unclear; hints in various letters suggest he might have fallen while repairing the roof of the stable, or that there was a riding accident in which his horse was killed. For several weeks it was possible that he would die, but even when his survival seemed assured it was clear that his recovery would take a long time and the family was in desperate need of money. So Angelo left again for America, departing Naples on March 10, 1910, having borrowed money from his cousin Clarice Vasquenz, his cousin (or uncle) Antonio Meogrossi, and his sister Pasquccia. At this point the oldest son Tommaso was already in America and the youngest, Agostino, was in prison in Viterbo.

In addition to Antonio's injury, his wife suffered from edema (water retention in the torso) and their daughter Pasquccia was dying from some form of infectious hepatitis. The burden of carrying on the agricultural affairs therefore fell on the other daughter, Mariuccia. Antonio did recover in time, although he continued to complain of pain and shortness of breath for another year. Angelo's debt to Pasquccia weighed greatly on Antonio's mind and he wrote several letters to his son during the first year begging him to repay the loan as his top priority, so that Pasquccia could provide for her little daughter Marietta.

When Antonio was close to death, he arranged to transfer his interest in the fields and other assets to his wife. This led to considerable bad feeling on the part of Pasquccia's husband Giovanni, who had been promised a share in the fields as part of the dowry when they married. According to Antonio, when Giovanni returned in fall of 1910 and realized that his wife was dying, he pressured her relentlessly in hopes of forcing Antonio to keep his promise. But Antonio refused, arguing that he would have no way to support himself were he to surrender the fields. Indeed at that point much of the produce had already been sequestered by some of his creditors. As a result, when Pasquccia died in spring of 1911 there was a series of arguments, culminating in Giovanni and Antonio mutually refusing to have anything to do with each other.

Angelo sent back money periodically, probably by electronic transfer to the bank, usually in amounts of 100-400 *lire* (roughly equivalent to $400 to $1500 today, Appendix II). Although he and Antonio occasionally disagreed on the best use of these funds, in general Antonio respected his wishes and conscientiously reported how he had used them. The uses include wages for day workers and plowmen, payments for seed grain, village taxes, the annual rent for the fields, loans from the bank, fees to notaries and lawyers for preparing documents, and unspecified debts to individuals. All of the debts involved interest payments, which ran as high as 20%.

It seems probable that Angelo had already decided he would not be returning to Cerchio, for in late 1910 he asked Antonio to find out how he could formally renounce all financial interest in his father's affairs. It took Antonio a while to get the information, but in the end he learned that it could only be done after his death. He and his wife therefore decided to make a will leaving their goods to Angelo and the imprisoned Agostino, pointedly disinheriting the delinquent Tommaso, who never wrote or sent money. This caused frequent trouble between Tommaso and Angelo in America, although they seem to have made it up each time.

In August 1911 disaster struck when several creditors sequestered Antonio's produce. This was not a new experience for him; at
the end of 1910 there had been a similar sequestration. But in this
case Antonio was convinced that his creditors were in the wrong
and filed suit (in his wife's name, since she was now the titular
owner) to request a reconsideration. Here he descended into the
morass of the Italian legal system (see Chapter 5). The case dragged
on for almost two years before it was heard, being put on the docket and postponed a total of nine times. Each time he had to pay a
fee for the docketing, a fee to the lawyer, and make some "presents"
to witnesses for taking the time to appear. Moreover, he was unable
to sell the sequestered produce or even get any for family consumption without paying a fee. But, with typical *contadino* stub-
bornness, he refused to settle out of court, convinced that he would
be vindicated. In spring 1912 yet another consequence arose: the
local manager for the Torlonia Administration told Antonio that
he would lose his title to the fields if he were unable to pay at least
the annual rent. Fortunately, Angelo was able to come through
with the needed funds. The case was finally heard in spring of 1913
but at that point the magistrate asked for a copy of the original order to distrain, and we never learn the result of the case.

In September 1912 Antonio urged Angelo to scrape up any
money he could, "even at the cost of getting a loan", so that they
could pay off the mortgage on his house. The creditor had been
threatening to buy up all of their other IOUs and then foreclose.
With a stupendous effort, Angelo did so and in November 1912 the
mortgage was paid in full with Angelo's uncle Carmine acting as
his proxy. Although the mortgage principal was only 400 *lire*, the
incidental fees added up to another 225 *lire*, leaving them still
slightly behind.

The letter series ends in summer of 1913, with the crops destroyed by drought, the case still undecided, and the stable roof
threatening to fall in. The major debts have all been paid off,
thanks to Angelo's labors, but there are always the need for wages
for the field workers and loans for seed grain. A final letter two

years later indicates that one of the brothers had died, and that Mariuccia's husband Vincenzo had returned to Italy and was serving at the Italian front.

Chapter 9
ANTONIO'S LETTERS[61]

The first letter was written when Angelo was still at sea, dictated by Antonio to his niece Marietta. Antonio was in too much pain to write and his wife and daughter were illiterate. The initial letters are very brief, providing only an update on Antonio's health. On March 31st his daughter Mariuccia adds some comments, expressing her anxiety at having to manage affairs on her own. In the very first letter, despite his own distress, Antonio reminds his son of the need to repay Pasquccia for the loan. This will become a constant theme during 1910, as will the difficulty caused by the loss of the mare.

> My very dear sons,   March 13, 1910
>   I write this letter to give you our news. We have pretty good health, thank God, as I hope to learn is the same for you and Rosa. My dears, I am still the same, with no improvement. The doctor told me that if another illness isn't added I will have recovered a bit in another two months from now, but only if I don't get pneumonia like the pleurisy I've already had. They still haven't strapped me up and it will be another 15 days before they do. I hope that all this won't happen. I hope to recover as soon as possible. If God wills, I'll be better in a future letter. For now I don't have any more to tell you, I just warn you to watch out for your health...
>
> PS. Dear son Angelo, Remember you-know-what about Pasquccia's affairs

---

[61] The ellipsis (...) indicates omitted material, mostly standardized salutations and closing statements. Italicized words in brackets are those we have not been able to read clearly or that don't make sense.

My dear sons,   March 31, 1910
    I'm letting you know that my cure will take a long time.
The doctor has said that there is no risk of death any more but
it will be more than a month for me to recover. I have to stay
in bed without being able to move or turn over to right or left
even a little, always flat on my back. I hope to tell you about it,
but who knows?...

PS. This is your sister to greet you warmly along with Rosa,
and to let you know that our father's illness will take a long
time because he's suffering atrocious pains all along his left
side. We hope he'll be able to get up around the middle of
April, but it's very unlikely that he'll even be able to come with
me to carry out business matters. We must get them done. I
would be very glad if he could come with me if only as a guide
and for company but the fact is that even if he did get up he
couldn't accompany me because we can't get a draft animal[62]
from Santucci because he wants at least half the price. There
are many other things I should tell you but since I'm expecting
your letter within a few days I will let you know everything in
my reply. Dearest brothers, as to our mother she is feeling just
as unwell as when you left, as is true also for our sister Pasquccia.

P.S. Antonetta sends you many kisses. She still has problems
with her eyes

By early April the family has heard from Angelo, who was able
to send a small amount of money. Antonio is beginning his slow
recovery and is considerably more verbose, although he is still dic-
tating the letters to his niece Marietta. He urges Angelo to send
more money as soon as possible to pay off a bank loan and to buy
another draft animal, and if possible also to send a little money for
the youngest son, Agostino, who is in prison. Antonio's personality

---

[62] *Bestia* is translated here as "draft animal". *Contadini* use the word to refer to farm
animals in general. From context, Antonio is probably thinking of a horse or mule, so I
have used "draft animal" throughout to avoid specifying more closely.

begins to emerge as he complains about the lack of financial and emotional support from various relatives.

Very Dear Son,   April 6, 1910
    I received your letter with five *lire* inside which have been really beneficial to me because what you left is all used up, and also a few *lire* for Mariuccia...
    As to my illness, for ten days or more I've been in constant danger of death and unconscious. Now there's no more danger of death, but I'm still in bed, crucified with pains, without being able to move at all. Today I got up for about a quarter of an hour, but I couldn't hold myself upright any more and had to go back to bed. Your mother has the familiar pains at present, because she had to sacrifice herself and she is still sacrificing herself for me, along with Mariuccia, and if it weren't for Mariuccia I can say that I might be dead.
    As to the bank, you already know it's a dangerous matter. If you can, try to make up for it. As to the draft animal, it's extremely necessary. I've had Mariuccia speak to Santucci about it twice. She replied that he wants at least half the money on delivery. As to the stable and other things, as you already know I will try to do the most I can to protect myself from the blows they may give me. Meanwhile, you do what you said and let it be at once.
    As to Clarice, she wasn't willing to give me anything. On the contrary, I tell you that from the day of your departure none of our relatives have to come to my house any more to visit me, and above all our relative who lives above the station. I remember seeing her only one time, at that moment when I was almost in the other world. Very well, that's how she rewarded the kindness that I did her when I could. And your Aunt Costanza had the barbaric nerve on March 12th to come to the house and make a very strong appeal to me because of the little IOUs[63] that your uncle Carmine signed with me. She should not have done that, but rather she should have thought about the situation I was in. But I consider it a strong obligation and I will try to discharge it if I can. Grazia Mione would give me as much wine as I want, but I can't drink the old wine and she won't give me the new in large amounts, and so this

---

[63] *Cambiale* = promissory note. I've used IOU as an informal term throughout.

far I have taken only three flasks of unfermented wine at six *soldi*,64 but I don't like it much. I must try to get myself about thirty liters of the fermented.

I'm letting you know that your mother has decided that she wants to go to the celebration of the Madonna della Libera and if I'm well it's fitting that I go also but 12 or 13 *lire* will go away; if you can think of us you will do well. I would have so many other things to tell you, but I will tell you when I can write. I move on to give you greetings from your mother, from Mariuccia and from Pasquccia – she implores you about you-know-what, her illness still continues as before......

Here's Agostino's address for you if you send him something. All is charity, it's written in the doctrine to visit those imprisoned – To: Sig. Vasquenz Augusto, prisoner in the jail of Viterbo, Roma Province.

A brief note one week later, revealing that Antonio tries to save postage costs by enclosing his letters with those being sent by relatives to others working in Pennsylvania. The few envelopes preserved with the letters, and several comments therein, suggest that the men shared a post office box in Pennsylvania. He's still waiting for the money.

Dear Son,   April 13, 1910
I sent you a note by way of a letter to Vincenzo Pantano, now I'm sending this one in a letter from Grazia Mione to let you know that I can't say I'm perfectly well, but I thank God a thousand times that, although I still can't leave the bed because the pains keep increasing, I hope that in a few days [too faded to read]. Meanwhile, I can say that I'm well in comparison to how I was, and how I might have been.

It's been three days now that I've been waiting for what you sent to the bank but nothing has come and what is worse, we've finished everything we had to eat, and everything for the fire...

PS: I'm letting you know that it's been very cold around here from April 2 until two days ago, always with a strong *tramon-*

---

64 See Weights and Measures. One *soldo* is five centimes or 1/20 of a *lira*, similar to the American nickel

tana and rain and snow, and this cold may be the reason for the delay in my getting well. Let's hope the warmth will come quickly and my life will get a bit easier.

By early May Antonio is back in form, and considerably annoyed that Angelo is taking so long to send money. The planting season is advancing and he urgently needs money to pay field workers, especially since he is still too incapacitated to do anything himself. Nobody else does the work to his satisfaction anyway. This letter also gives the first indication of the friction with the oldest son, Tommaso. Throughout the letters it becomes evident that Angelo is the favored son, and Tommaso has always been difficult.

> Dear Son,   May 6, 1910
> The third of this month I got your letter which I had been expecting for about a month, certainly before now, but since he who is beating on my head doesn't make any mistakes,[65] the person who told everyone before he left that he would level a mountain, leaving behind country and parents, refuses even to split a turnip. I have sent you several notes by way of Vincenzo Pantano and Grazia Mione, informing you that we have used up the firewood, the food, and the money, and since in your first letter you told me that I should try to get another draft animal, I explained everything, not only in those notes but also in the reply to your first letter, and I told you that Santucci wants at least half the money before he will sell me an animal. Money is what I don't have, and why he hasn't given me an animal yet, and that is what I need most, because we can't lose even one day in the Bacinetto. I sent Francesco Zecchino, a capable man, to plant the beets, but he planted them deeper than the potatoes and they haven't sprouted yet. I sent Quiloli to plant potatoes and he went along skin-deep as if they had been fennel. I can't tell you what a mess the grain is – poppies, vetch, alfalfa – they tell me that seventy days of work wouldn't be enough to clear it, and the women want 30 *soldi*. I don't

---

[65] most likely translation of "*ma siccome che quello che zappa alla testa mia non sbaglia niente*". An alternative translation might be "although I work the soil I don't make mistakes in my head". Either way, he must have changed his thought in the middle of the sentence.

know where to turn to have the wine cleaned, and I haven't been able to send anyone, first because I have to get the money to pay them, and second because of the bad weather; it's been raining continuously. What can Mariuccia do all by herself? She does so much, everything rests on her shoulders. Your mother is still in bad health, with the same pain in her side and between the suffering and anxiety I can say she's almost completely lost her hearing.

Now let me give you a clear description of my health, because in the reply that Grazia Mione sent you she said that I was perfectly recovered. That was so as not to worry you, here is the true story: from the day of the accident to the sixth day the doctor said I was certainly dying. After that day, because there was an unexpected change, he said, "There are two more days of danger, because of pneumonia." After those days he said, "We have also conquered the pneumonia. We can hope that he will get well." The twelfth day he released me, saying "Now there's no more I can do for you, because the fever has also passed. As for the pains, there's no need for medicine because they are muscular." But because the pains changed and I had a new pain under the ribs on the left as far as the stomach, and a chest so swollen it looked like a drumhead, I called the doctor again. He came, very arrogant. I told him I had a swollen stomach; he replied haughtily, "It's from eating too much". A few more days passed, the pain and breathlessness increased. I had to call him yet again, and he wouldn't come, although he was right next door at Elizabetta's house. Two days after he was called he came on his own, then he examined me minutely and found that the swelling was from water and air in the body, so he said, "There's nothing I can do for you about this, it has to go away by itself. Start getting up and walk as much as you can." So I began to get up, but after I walked about twenty steps the swelling increased and I couldn't breathe, so I had to throw myself back on the bed in agony, or sit on two chairs with cushions behind my shoulders. It's already been two months since the day of my accident and the pain and breathlessness are the same as before. I went to the Madonna della Libera, but I could barely manage to go from the station to the church without having to rest in the street.66 To cut it short

---

66 Apparently in another town, so that they took the train.

because this seems too boring, suffice it to say that your mother has to dress me in the morning and undress me at night. If the Lord God and the Most Holy Virgin of Grace grant me a complete cure, that's fine. If not, it would be better to die; I'd be doubly happy not to stay on earth a few more days so impaired, without being able to earn even a penny a day. As for clearing the grain, I could barely do something on my knees, resting one hand on the ground, but who would take me there?

Now let me say that we are all glad that you all enjoy the best of health, but I tell you again as I said at the beginning of this letter, that you should not act in future as you have so far – after leaving your father dying you dragged out two months before writing. We thought it was some terrible accident, but instead it was just your foot-dragging. You should write at least every 15 days, otherwise it's a sign that you want to be far away in thought as you are in person. I can't believe you want to be one of those ill-willed people. At most you should know the position I'm in. I say nothing of the family's needs because you can imagine it from what's above. You should know that as of today I've eaten one hen, two and a half kilos of meat, and otherwise I've made do with some eggs, and all for lack of money.

I won't go on any more.... On my behalf greet Tommaso and tell him that as soon as my brother Isidoro and my nephew Enrico learned of my accident they sent me a sympathy letter with 15 *lire* to help me,[67] while he, my flesh-and-blood son, was more pleased than polite. It's said around Cerchio that he sent a note of congratulations, that he wasn't sorry about my accident. I don't say that he should do as Isidoro and Enrico did, but I craved a simple note of greeting, to let me know his regret. So just tell him I'm sorry about this.

By early May Angelo has managed to send a substantial sum of money. Antonio has been able to pay a tax to the village, but could only pay the interest on the bank loans, which had to be renegotiated. Most of the money was used for food and fuel and Antonio, rather ungratefully, reminds his son that he still needs to pay the field workers for plowing. Money for the imprisoned Agostino

---

[67] These two men were in Cleveland, Ohio at the time (1910 census).

would be appreciated, and the debt to Pasquccia remains important.

> Undated, probably early May 1910
>
> I'm sending you the devotions of the Madonna della Libera. Do a few for each of us. I, your mother, your sister Pasquccia and Antonetta went to the Madonna. The trip was very successful. Your sister implores you for you-know-what, so that she won't have any reproaches, and I also implore you for something for us. In your letter I would have wanted at least some twenty *lire* to pay those of the Colonica family to break the land in the Bacinetto.
>
> I got the 100 *lire*, I paid 30 *lire* to the town and the rest was consumed for the family. For the two payments due to the bank I could only pay the interest, and I had one carried over to July first, and the other to August 20th.
>
> You asked for Agostino's address. I sent it to you, I repeat it again: Prisoner in the Jail of Viterbo, Prov. Rome. Send him something, I don't say as a brother but at least as a neighbor. Recall the words of the *Misericordia Corporale*[68] that say: Visit the sick, visit the imprisoned, and bury the dead. I believe that in America they make some charitable gifts, and you instead will do it for your brother. All is charity. I can't send him even a cent because I find myself in the most extreme state of inability...
>
> I repeat many greetings to you, and to all, and I repeat myself because I don't trust myself to write any more. To get this letter done I've written it over two days, a little at a time.

A confusing note which unfortunately deals with an important topic: the mutual debts with Pasquccia's husband Giovanni. It seems that at the time of the marriage Antonio was unable to pay a dowry, and in fact was in need of money himself. It was therefore

---

[68] A list of acts of charity derived from Matthew 25:35-36, "...for I was hungry and you gave me food, I was thirsty and you gave me drink, I was a stranger and you welcomed me, I was naked and you clothed me, I was sick and you visited me, I was in prison and you came to me." The Catholic Church defines seven bodily acts (*misericordia corporale*) and seven spiritual acts (*misericordia spirituale*) required to obtain forgiveness and enter into Heaven.

agreed that Giovanni would loan his new father-in-law 200 *lire*, to be repaid by Antonio's signing over some of the Fucino fields to Giovanni. However, Antonio never did transfer the fields, pleading that he would have no other source of income. Nor did he repay the 200 *lire*. Moreover, when Angelo left for America he borrowed a further 200 *lire* from his sister Pasquccia, leaving the Vasquenz family with a net 400-*lire* debt to Pasquccia and Giovanni. The note below suggests that at some point, probably while the men were in America, Giovanni borrowed some money from Angelo. Here Antonio wants to know if any of the latter has been repaid; if not, it could be deducted from the family's 400-*lira* debt. Antonio's greatest concern is that Pasquccia's loan to her brother be repaid before she dies. He was apparently writing in haste, interrupting himself as thoughts occurred, so that the text is somewhat opaque. (Other letters in the collection indicate that Angelo did send the 200 *lire* that he owed to Pasquccia in August 1910, but that the original 200-*lire* loan was never repaid, leading to much bitterness after Pasquccia's death.)

Dear son,   Undated, May or June 1910
this note is only for you
 Do me the pleasure to let me know by return post what is your situation as to accounts with your brother-in-law Giovanni for the money that he was supposed to pay back to you, because I should have given him an IOU for the 200 *lire* that he gave me when he got married. If he has withdrawn something, let me know so that we can make up the IOU with Pasquccia while she is alive, if it comes in time, because the sickness is increasing and the doctor has told several people who asked that it's impossible she can get through the month of June. So reply by return post – and it would also be good if you could repay her the money that you owe so that she can leave her affairs on a solid footing, even if you have to get a loan – and remit them to her by telegram. For now, tell her husband that the sickness has increased. Don't make it sound too dangerous, but he will certainly have to know soon. Let's hope in the Lord that it will not be. I renew my greetings and don't fail to do what I've said, the money [to be sent] in the name of Mariuccia.

Another confusing letter; clarifications are inserted in brackets. Antonio explains that when it was believed he might die after his accident he transferred his tenancy rights in the Fucino fields to his wife Maria Domenica. The transfer was arranged by their Senate Deputy, Carlo Costanzi, who also arranged for a "subsidy" to be paid to Maria Domenica. However, the fields had been previously promised to the son-in-law Giovanni as part of the dowry (see letter above), and Antonio was told that he might have to get Giovanni's agreement to transfer the fields to Maria Domenica. He was therefore forced to inform Angelo and Giovanni what he was planning. Apparently Giovanni wrote an angry letter in which he threatened to send Antonio to jail. This makes it all the more imperative that Angelo repay the loan from Pasquccia, and Antonio includes a separate note to that effect. Several letters indicate that the family did not want Giovanni to learn how desperate Pasquccia's condition was, although they were finally forced to tell him later in the summer.

Dear Son,   June 7, 1910
    I reply to your letter with very urgent promptness. I am glad that you, like Tommaso and Rosa, enjoy perfect health, as do the two brothers-in-law. As to our health I can't tell you anything good, because I still have pains in the ribs and side so that I can't do anything. The crops will be lost because I can't cultivate them, the daily wages cost a lot and there's no money to pay them. Or to say it better: we have enough food for eight days, and after that we'll have to go around the countryside gathering plants in order to live. Your mother's health is much weaker than before, the pains that she suffered before are doubled, and throughout the countryside no one can do anything, and especially we must get used to walking all the time. Mariuccia is in reasonable health but too much tiredness makes her discouraged because she's alone. Then as to the health of Pasquccia I say nothing because I told you in my last letter before this one; I will just say that the illness is getting much worse. I will include a little note with this, and it is only for you.

Now I move on to tell you about the Fucino fields, because in order to put them in your mother's name I used Carlo Costanzi, the Deputy, as middleman, because they [apparently some local officials] told Sperra [official for the Torlonia Administration] that it was no longer at their discretion to make these changes, but instead I must go to the General Administration in Rome for everything, and they didn't know if they would approve it or not. As soon as I learned that the matter was uncertain, I immediately thought of selling all the products of this year's harvest, declaring in the document that the said products were transferred to him [Costanzi] as refund for the subsidy that she received during my long illness, and whatever else she had to administer for me. I was told that perhaps spousal authorization would be needed [from Giovanni], and that's why I had asked for the letter from that brute, boor that he is, and then it got back to me from an astute person [Angelo] who wrote that he [Giovanni] was upset with me. Tell him on my behalf that he should learn to think things over before writing. Furthermore, he wrote that if my daughter was dying he would send me to prison. I would be very eager to visit a son in jail [a reference to Agostino], but I wish I'd had that shameless man in my hands when I read the note he sent me, and I swear to you by the Blessed Madonna that I would have butchered him like a young goat. I would say many other things about the letter he wrote to Mariuccia, but I let it go in order not to get all stirred up again. I will only say that I treated him just like a pig and not a son-in-law, and this is only for his bad behavior in writing.

P.S. Don't let anyone know anything about the note I'm enclosing so that Giovanni doesn't learn about it.
P.P.S. I beg you, don't fail to carry out everything that has been written in the note enclosed. Promptness as fast as possible, farewell, farewell.

The included note, reminding Angelo of Pasquccia's own generosity to him:

Dear Son,
The urgency that I've had in replying to you has been for your sister Pasquccia. I implore you fervently to do the most

you possibly can and make Pasquccia happy. I should implore you for myself because as I have told you in the letter I have nothing to eat, and can't cultivate things through lack of money, but I don't care about myself so much as I'm concerned about her. Consequently, if you have pity on her as she has had for you, and if you want her to stay on this earth a few more days – if she gets through the month of June, or she may die even earlier – I beg you don't make her suffer. As soon as you receive this, I beg you to get some loan and send us the money immediately by telegram, either addressed to me or to Mariuccia. I implore you, don't make her live in suffering these few last days that are left to us. Since she must die don't let her die unhappy, because she wants to arrange for her daughter with this money if it comes in time. She begs you for the love of God and of the Blessed Virgin to do her this kindness. Indeed her illness is getting worse through thinking about this. With tears in her eyes she greets you lovingly, doubting not that this may be the last that she sends you. Farewell

Another plea for Pasquccia, containing one of two cases in which Antonio attempts to manipulate someone in Cerchio via a letter to be sent from one of the men in America. Pasquccia is dying at the house of her in-laws, and Antonio wants Giovanni to tell his mother to sleep with her in order to take better care of her.

Dear Son,   Undated, prior to Sept. 1910
    As to your sister Pasquccia, try to do the most you possibly can because believe me, she's really left without anything and she doesn't have a way to follow the treatment for lack of money, and the illness is increasing a good deal. She must stay in bed, and the mother doesn't want to sleep together, and if she is in the back room how can she know if there is some need? Tell Giovanni to write his mother that she should at least sleep, if not together in the bed, then at least on a straw pallet nearby, but without letting her know that he knows she doesn't want to sleep there, because then she will guess I wrote it, and she's capable of getting upset with Pasquccia. He should write her like this: "Dear Mother, given that for now Pasquccia's illness is not being cured and because she's been ill a long time, I want to know if you sleep together, or separate. If you

are separate, then I absolutely want you at least to sleep near her on a straw pallet if you don't want to sleep in the bed with her and so on," saying whatever else he wants to say. And tell Giovanni to send back something, and if he wants to do better, to send it by telegram so that it comes faster, because she has much need.

In late July Angelo managed to send the 200 *lire* to Pasquccia by way of Mariuccia. Apparently at some previous point he had also sent his father 200 *lire*, which he intended to be used to pay off one of his own debts. Antonio, however, used it for other purposes, and here he indignantly describes his pressing expenses, adding that he had to get another loan from the bank. The total harvest was ten *salme*, but that includes alfalfa seeds, which must be removed by winnowing, so the actual return of grain is only seven *salme*. This letter also gives us the clues to infer that Pasquccia's illness was from infectious hepatitis.

Dear Son,   August 15, 1910
    On the 11th I got your letter in which I see that you enjoy the best of health, as you have said your brothers-in-law do also. We are all well, but I am still not fully restored, and I never will be because the internal pains never cease. I keep going in the countryside only for overwhelming necessities. Your mother suffers the familiar pains every now and then.
    I note your complaints, saying that you sent me the 200 *lire* for that pig of San Berardo. I recall having written you these exact words in my note: "Send what you owe to Pasquccia and don't worry about me, even though I don't have a nickel. I used the 200 *lire* you sent to pay the bank, which fell due on March 12. I bought a donkey and gave 25 *lire* on account and must pay another 35 *lire*. My illness cost me about 250 *lire*, and otherwise I've spent them for labors of the countryside and for the reaping. The money you gave me to pay 115 *lire* of reaping went for reaping in the Bacinetto, not counting what Mariuccia and I did." You say it's my feelings (I had to turn to the bank and take out another 100 *lire*) because this year I had to pay the reapers from five to nine and a half *lire* per day, plus

all expenses. I recovered 10 *salme*[69] of grain and alfalfa; when it's winnowed it will be 7 – not enough to pay the rent – and not even one *coppa* has come back to the house. So you shouldn't be annoyed that I wrote you that I don't have even a nickel, and yet I didn't ask anything of you. I wrote you about this to make you aware of my position, and you know it without my telling you because you know how I was when you left, in health as well as the financial situation. I'm just annoyed by the inconvenience left from my illness so that I can't earn my bread without this daily coming and going and at least I would certainly earn food for me and your mother. But then, very rare are those who have died of hunger.

As to Pasquccia's health, the illness is always advancing, always getting worse. All the people who have this illness she has are already in the other world. Five days ago Antonio Cimini died, and today Brother, or rather the priest, Don Francesco died. And so if Pasquccia gets through one month she won't last another and she will have the same passage. She's become as yellow as saffron, and her face has also begun to swell. We hope in God, but I can tell you that if she gets well, the dead can rise, and doctor Gasbarre told me very clearly that the illness has gone on too long, and that after such a length she must either get well or she must die, and so she can't last much longer.

Giovanni finally learned of the seriousness of Pasquccia's illness and returned precipitately in September.[70] Apparently Angelo asked him to mediate with some of his creditors in Italy; several other letters indicate that Angelo and Giovanni had been boyhood friends and remained close despite the problems with Antonio. The nature of the debt to the notary is unknown, but it appears that the notary was serving as an intermediary in paying a tax in Avezzano, and there has been a confusion because Angelo paid the tax directly rather than going through the notary.

---

[69] For *salma* and *coppa* see Weights and Measures

[70] Mentioned by Giovanni in a letter to Angelo dated Jan. 22, 1911 in which he also mentions Antonio's refusal to part with the Fucino fields and asks Angelo to intervene for him.

Dear Son,   Sept. 25, 1910

I got your letter on the 17th of this month. I'm glad to see that you enjoy excellent health. We are also well in all ways, in health as in everything else. As for the problem between you and Tommaso, you may well recall that I have told you many times that you two have never gotten along, so each of you should try to think of your own affairs and that way you'll avoid any problems. Giovanni has come back in good health. Pasquccia is always the same; her illness is very serious. The proverb says "while there's life there's hope", but as for me I am out of hope, although it's said that God can bring back the dead, so let's hope that that is true.

I've received several notes from the notary in Celano, and the one included here is the most recent. From what he says he claims the entire hundred *lire*; he says that we should not have paid the tax collector because he says that what we gave the tax collector was a surtax that he sent him.

As for your request that I remind Giovanni to speak to Francesco Perille, I haven't told him anything yet because I only saw him once before receiving your letter and haven't seen him since, but I will tell him. Try to come to an agreement as best you can by giving a little to each of the people you know of no later than the end of September. The most important one is Davide Ciaglia of Collarmele to whom I indebted myself for the interest and I just don't have any way to raise a penny of it. I should tell you the whole position I'm in, but it would be useless. I will have to do what Nicola Ciaglia used to say whenever something strange happened to him (he said: where you fall, you fall and where you die, you die) and that's what I must do because there is no way to make up for little debts with a bad harvest...

PS Write a letter to the notary and send him the 50 *lire* and a bit, and tell him you paid the rest – the registration fee – to the collector of Avezzano. The notary's address is: Signor Notary Don Giovanni Alfonsi, Via dietro Castello, Celano.

I implore you to be prompt as to the above, because they won't give us any time. It would be good if you could repay the interest to Davide Ciaglia, and something on account for the big principal, and that would serve to renew the IOU and cancel your signature. Let me repeat my greetings, and about the promptness. (I wanted to write as soon as I received the letter from the notary, but I put it off until today in order to wait for your letter).

By late November Angelo has managed to send 350 *lire* and Antonio carefully details how he has distributed it among the creditors. The letters are somewhat unclear, but it appears that Carmine d'Alessandro held a mortgage jointly signed by Antonio and Angelo. Later letters reveal that he threatened to foreclose, and only in November 1912 were they able to pay him off. The other creditors receive interest and partial payments of the principal due them. Beyond that, the plowers must be paid, and a fee paid to redeem produce that has been sequestered from the fields that are now in Maria Domenica's name (Antonio usually speaks of the fields as his, but when convenient his wife is pushed to the fore.)

Dear Son,   November 25, 1910
    I reply to your letter with a few days delay to give you an accounting of how I've spent the money you sent. As you know, I've given 70 *lire* to Carmine d'Alessandro for the rent, or rather the interest, and I haven't yet given him the interest of 30 *lire* for which I signed an IOU, and he claims yet another 70 *lire* for a surtax that the tax collector imposed, and we are in disagreement about this because I don't intend to pay him for it. I paid Davide Ciaglia 16 *lire* for the interest, and 22.60 because he objected to an IOU. I've given the interest of 36.15 to Perille, and another twenty-five *lire* and 50 centimes on account for the principal, but he didn't want to receive them and Francesco Ramelli is keeping them on deposit. I've given Pizitto 50 *lire* on account and he told me that he's not satisfied. He may write you a note and tell you what he claims – reply to it as you like. I paid 27 *lire* to break the land in the Bacinetto, and I must pay 50 *lire* to the Chief of the Squad of S. Benedetto who sequestered the maize from Fucino. Although your mother could have filed a protest on the property, this goes through the warehouseman of the Administration, and so she didn't do it. And all this adds up to the sum of £299.25. For the other 50 *lire* and 75 centimes – you know very well about the family

need, and above all that we are really poor in everything this year, because we haven't recovered anything and so the rest went to pay other little debts; one *lira* here, five there, ten the other place, and so the 50 *lire* have been scattered around.

I would rather try to reduce the debt, dear son, and not increase it. Meanwhile, when you can send something back, do so and write to tell me whom I should give it to, and I will. I don't worry so much about our means of living, but I repeat that we have only about one more month of expenses from the maize, if that, and then we won't have anything else, and if we want to go out to borrow a spoonful of salt, or even for a pound of flour, we won't find it, but since your mother has taken about six [*decine di livori*] and fibers for spinning, and so someone gives us some ten of wheat, and another a quarter of vegetables and with this we live from day to day until we can go out to the countryside to earn something for ourselves, because now we are besieged first by a quantity of rain in the past, and on the evening of the 21st there was a blizzard – in two hours there was about 30 centimeters – and now it's nothing but heavy frosts and the snow is intact without melting at all, and what is worse, we haven't dug up the beets yet. If we manage not to die this year, then we never will. So as Nicola Ciaglia used to say, "Four loaves and a good flask and we'll take the world as it comes."...

Angelo sent another 50 *lire* in early December, not having received Antonio's letter above (comments in Antonio's letters indicate that mail was frequently delayed for several weeks). Antonio now claims to have forgotten one of the creditors in his previous distribution, and when the man came to demand his money Antonio hastily wrote another letter asking for more, as he explains here. He then moves on to a fascinating example of the kind of calculations that a farmer must make in deciding what crops to plant, explaining that sugar beets will give a better return than maize or wheat. The reasoning is a bit hard to follow: his key point is that even a small amount of beets (5 *coppe*) have produced 100 *lire*, enough to pay the rent on the land for a year, whereas both the grain reserved for next year's seed and that for sale must be sorted and sieved, resulting in a modest profit at best. High profit from the beets also allows him to indulge in a little maize, a much less efficient crop.

This letter also contains the first reference to Angelo's desire for a *rinuncia*, a legal renouncing of all interest in his father's finances. He is also trying to get a copy of the mortgage agreement with Carmine d'Alessandro, which is held by the notary.

Dear Son,   January 1, 1911

On the 29th of last month I got your letter of December 8, in which you reproach me for not replying to your last letter. As to all this, I tell you I barely got the letter with the £ 50 just a few days after the 300 *lire*, but hadn't touched it yet. As soon as I got the second one I distributed the money, and wrote you promptly after three or four days – I don't remember if it was the 25th or perhaps the 26th – and in it I gave a full account of how I spent the money. I still owed something to Pietro Alessandro and that's why I sent you the begging letter, because I didn't remember that little IOU for 36 *lire*. About ten days ago he came to Cerchio and then I remembered everything. He also told me that he had received a letter from you. At the time he came I couldn't give him anything and I told him to be patient and that he would get the interest for this year just as before, but he kept saying he wanted the £36 back. Everything else that I gave others was reported minutely in the letter that I sent you, as I said above. By the way, Pizitto wanted to put a note in the letter. If you really haven't received it let me know, and I will send the accounting again.

You also reproach me for planting beets.71 My dear boy, it's better for me to plant them every year, seeing that I'm delayed in my payments to the Administration – perhaps only a few, but not none at all. I've been very tired this year and I couldn't cultivate them when they needed it, because of my bad health. And yet 5 *coppe* of land have brought in 100 *lire*, and with that I can pay for one year's rent. Without that I couldn't get back those few ears of maize, because with the ten *salme* of grain that I replanted I recovered two *salme* to sow and 8 left over. But the fact is that the two *salme* for sowing

_____

71 Possibly because Angelo wanted his father to support the strike against the Roman Sugar Company (see Chapter 4)

yielded fourteen *coppe* after being sorted, while the eight *salme* after sieving at a 17 mesh[72] yielded six and a half. At 33 *lire* each, that's 214.30. I certainly couldn't get that profit either from the maize – or even the two *salme* for the sowing – if it weren't for those few beets. And so it's best for me always to plant them; as I said, at least a few, but not none at all. My only real disaster is that I don't have any draft animal. Hard work doesn't dismay me at all, but it increases the walking and that's why I have to postpone work in the countryside, because if I walk to the Bacinetto one day then I need three or four days to recuperate before I can go again, and all this is because of the problems resulting from that fall I had. Zincaro Santuccio has been keeping me hanging for a year now and he still hasn't been willing to give me a draft animal. Finally on Nov. 22 he said one would be ready but he wants at least half the money, and so I haven't been able to get around. And it would be the greatest necessity not only for me but even more for your mother who is always or almost always ill and can't give me any help because she can't walk, and also to bring back something for the fire, and so much else.

I went to the Notary as you asked me, and he wasn't there. I will go back after the holidays are over. As to the *rinuncia* I must first get some information and then I'll let you know.

The chief of the S. Benedetto squad confiscated the maize in the Bacinetto, and I couldn't make a complaint to him because it goes through the Manager of the warehouse. If it was some other person I couldn't manage it, but with him I had to stand firm because he could play me some trick with the fields.

Agostino keeps asking me for your address. Write to him some time, and send him some money. Everything is charity, and especially toward those in prison. I can't help him with even a cent.

We are in reasonably good health. Mariuccia is well, but it's unlikely her daughter will get well. It's three months now that she's been seriously ill. Pasquccia's illness is constantly getting worse, she may die before we realize it. Reply to this letter at once.

If you want to write to Agostino here is the address

---

[72] *che lasciai a 17 conciate col crivello*

Augusto Vasquenz, Prisoner in the Jail of Viterbo, Province Rome

Angelo has sent another installment and this time Antonio has paid it as requested. Cousin Clarice has been paid in full and Pizitto, who advanced seed grain for sowing last year, has been partially paid. A separate 50 *lire* has been used for down payment on a mare and interest to the mortgage-holder. But now a new crisis has arisen: Antonio has received a summons for immediate payment of the money due for seed grain, 100 *lire*. The official had previously sequestered the produce from the fields and is now pushing for payment, otherwise he threatens to cancel Antonio's contract with the Torlonia Administration. Antonio apologizes in advance, knowing that Angelo is getting annoyed by the constant demands. He moves on to assure his son that he is trying to get some needed information from a notary and then gives a vivid picture of the family health problems. Mariuccia's daughter Antonetta is at death's door and may have died shortly after this letter. Touchingly, Mariuccia paid for a family photograph to send to her husband, Vincenzo di Domenico, who is working in the mines with Angelo.

Dear son,   February 26, 1911
    I reply to your letter after a delay of twelve days. I delayed so long to wait for the money to arrive. It reached me the 23rd of this month, and I have distributed it exactly as you said, and neither Clarice nor even Pizitto were willing to leave me a cent. I settled the debt with Pizitto in cash, and gave him 25 *lire* on account for the debt of 26 *coppe* of grain. Now 18 *coppe* of the grain is left, because I gave him 8 *coppe* of it for a good reason, so he couldn't demand interest on what is left for this year but only for the 18 *coppe*, as he has already written you in his note, and be sure to keep it because he might misunderstand and make us pay the whole 26 *coppe*.
    As to the 50 *lire* that you sent me, I barely received it when I had to send 35 *lire* to Santuccio, half the price of a mare that I went to get 15 days ago today, because it was impossible to go without a draft animal, and I have to give him another 35 *lire* on August 26. I gave six *lire* for interest to Pietro

70

d'Alessandro of Collarmele, and I've paid eight *lire* for the moveable goods of Fucino. One *lira* is left for me, but there are already distraints on the lands. So many other things to pay, and your mother has worn out all the shoes you left, and now she can't go out because she is literally barefoot, with only socks. But there's something much worse: the chief of the squadron has summonsed me for the entire amount, which would be 100 *lire*, and I've asked for two months of time. He did this premature summons in order to renew the sequestration from the Bacinetto. I could file a protest on behalf of your Mother and he would lose the costs, but since this goes through Sig. Domenico (the warehouseman) it's better for me to pay him, because the warehouseman could have even the land taken from me; he's already talked about it with the Representative,[73] letting him know that this is not a specific debt, but is for grain given for sowing in the Bacinetto. And so it's best for me to bow my head and pay him. I'm ashamed to speak to you in this way because you tell me that you're left high and dry, and don't have much work, but I should certainly let you know the full position of our family. There is more to tell you but I'll pass over it so as not to upset you because to everything I say you reply "Why must I think about these payments?" And so I don't tell you about it, except that this year we have had a sorry harvest and have nothing. But it doesn't matter to stay alive because we go from day to day, and we eat. But the bad thing is what we must pay, and now we don't have even a nickel of credit because no one will give it to me. My other thought is to pay the daily wages [or day workers] for the vaccine that I must keep in the Fucino.[74]

Now let's leave this rigmarole because it's lengthy. You spoke of the notary; I've gone to Celano twice expressly to see him and never found him in. I'll go back as soon as possible. As to the *rinuncia*, I haven't got the information about it yet, because until now I haven't had the means to go to a lawyer.

---

[73] Sperra, the local representative of the Torlonia Administration

[74] *l'aldro mio pensiero è per pagare le giornate dell Vaccine che debbo tenere a fucino.* This looks like a definite reference to animal vaccinations, unless it refers to a person named Vaccine. There is no other indication that Antonio keeps farm animals like cattle that would need a vaccine. Possibly anyone using the animal waste as fertilizer was expected to contribute to their treatments.

I'll let you know in another letter, but I think it comes at a time after my death.

I see from your letter that you enjoy the best of health. I'm glad of it. As to our health, we aren't ill but neither can we say that we have perfect health, because your mother still has the visceral pains, and a swollen belly, and I have the inconvenience of that damned shortness of breath left over from the illness after my accident. After a year now there are so many things I can't do without getting tired, and walking increases it a lot. It's so bad that if I go to the Bacinetto once on foot I have to take care of myself for two or three days without being able to do anything.

Mariuccia is well in health, but the anxiety she has for Antonetta is like a double sickness for her. The girl has been ill for five months, and for four months she hasn't been able to get up from the cradle. With her face, and swollen belly, and arms and thighs it's gotten so that she looks like a little stalk of hemp when you take off the compress. She can't sit up any more, and for the last eight days she hasn't eaten. She lives on water, milk and medicine, and with all this she has a tongue that grates on everyone who hears her. If this illness passes and is resolved it will really be a miracle, as it would be a miracle if Pasquccia gets well. But the Father Eternal will do no more miracles and so neither one nor the other can get well because they are always getting worse.

Mariuccia sends her photograph and one of Antonetta. Mariuccia came out with her mouth open, but that was because she was starting to speak to the girl because she wouldn't sit still. Pasquccia wanted to get photographed, but she couldn't for lack of money. Mariuccia wouldn't have made this expense either, but to let her father [Antonetta's father, Vincenzo] see her, and also because if she dies she wants to keep it as a memory.

I won't go on any more because it's late and I'm sleepy...I don't know how you're doing with your brother Tommaso. If you're getting along with him, give him many, many greetings from me. I hope you are getting along, but I doubt it. Nonetheless, let me know about him, and let me know how he is...

Pasquccia finally dies on March 10, 1911 and Antonio pours out his grief and also his anger with Pasquccia's husband Giovanni and his mother, whom he accuses of hastening her death by negligence. Antonio believes, probably correctly, that Giovanni was attempting to blackmail him into paying the long-overdue dowry. Giovanni then told the woman who was laying out the body to take the gold earrings from Pasquccia's ears, but Antonio discovered the ruse and demanded that they be returned. In revenge, Giovanni planned to exclude his in-laws from the *riuscita*, probably the formal procession from the home to the church for the funerary mass. Antonio learned about it in time, but the upshot of everything is that Giovanni wants nothing more to do with the Vasquenz family. Angelo and Giovanni are best friends, and Antonio warns his son never to trust Giovanni again.

Dear son,   March 17, 1911

With the greatest regret of our whole family, I send you the unhappy news of the death of your sister Pasquccia on the tenth of this month, at half past noon, comforted by all the divine sacraments. Her blessed soul rests peacefully in the arms of the Lord, leaving us afflicted and inconsolable for the loss of one so loved. But this is not the case for her mother-in-law and her husband, as I shall tell you all about it here. Meanwhile, console yourself as we have done, first because it was a beautiful death. I can say she died like an angel; in commending her soul she made the sign of the cross every time that the priest gave the benediction. Finally she asked how much longer it would be to die and exclaimed, "Oh, it's so long!" and at that moment she expired without any of us even realizing it.

For the second reason, I can assure you that they made her die of weakness and also of heartbreak, and we have consoled ourselves about this, and you must also convince and console yourself, because she has finished her suffering and troubles at the hands of those cruel people without heart or feelings. Now I move on to tell you all the heartless things that her husband and mother-in-law have done, not only in life but even after death. When her husband first came back, for a few days he took care of her as before, but when he realized that the illness was incurable he didn't take care of her any more. He didn't give her more than a nickels-worth of milk, a nickels-worth of wine, a half pound of meat. She was forced to eat as leftovers the same things they had, disdained by her husband and mother-in-law – the spoon, fork, plate, and a sip from a cup of water, without being able to get herself water from the *conca*75 and drink from the dipper; everything by gesture for fear lest they might take away half a kilo of maize and replace it with an apple or pear; left alone many, many days without their leaving anything for her to eat. Some days when your mother learned about it she would go and bring her something, and when she didn't know she spent the days without anything to eat. And so many, many other things that I'm leaving out. And why did he do this? Because he wanted her to force me to give him the two hundred *lire* and finish paying the dowry. If I had known all this at the time, as sick as she was I would have brought her home with me. She told everyone that they loved her and that she lacked for nothing, but she said this so as not to be totally abandoned. Suffice it to say that on the morning of the tenth she made confession, and after the communion was brought he left her of blessed memory almost dying, and went off to till the soil, without being present when she expired. She asked me many times if Giovanni had returned but what can I tell you? Upon returning he found her dead and wasn't man enough to look us in the face, or even shed a tear, neither he nor his mother. All he could think of was giving orders to Bazziere's daughter to take the earrings from her ears without our knowing, although she of blessed memory had many times implored Mariuccia, asking not to be abandoned, and that nothing would be taken off, but that she would be dressed as if she were leaving the house. Yet with all this, while she was putting her into the coffin, Bazziere's daughter had the nerve to pull the earrings from her ears. In the morning I broke open the coffin and seeing that they were missing I made her put them back.

And as if this weren't enough there is more to say, even more affecting, because that day it happened by chance that the priest had to perform two funerals, one for her of blessed memory and the other for Giuseppe Antidormi, or rather Pompei. There being only one priest he couldn't perform two functions, so he said to me, "Today I'll do the service for the dead man, and Monday for the woman, or if you prefer I'll apply today's mass for both, and the Monday mass also for both."

---

75 *conca* = A large earthenware jug used for storing water outside the house

I agreed, and let it be known by way of Brizio that the *riusci-ta*[76] could not be on Monday, because there was the funeral to be done. Brizio's reply was that the *riuscita* was being done on the seventh day. Late on Sunday he learned by chance that they were having the *riuscita* and since neither we nor any of our relatives [knew about it], in order to be certain I sent your cousin Marietta to ask him about it. Do you know what he replied? "I'm having the *riuscita* tomorrow. If it's not convenient for them, let them do it at their expense and their convenience." He and his witch of a mother had told only one or two of their relatives, without telling any of ours, just because of the earrings. And then he wanted those of our house and our relatives to come to his house to get him and bring him to the church! All this was not convenient for us. I did no more; I called a few relatives impromptu, and all our neighbors went to the mass and after leaving the church came back to the house. He got touchy about this and said that he doesn't want to be called one of us any more and that I should do what I could about the 200 *lire*.

I can write no more, and I beg you to read this several times because there are mistakes, and periods and commas are missing,[77] so you have to read it over several times. There are so many more things to say, but while I was writing they flew out of my mind. I just tell you not to treat him as a friend any more, or as a brother-in-law, but rather think of him as the first and greatest enemy in the world.

I want to tell you a proverb that the ancients said, and it's this: Never bring a man with red hair into the house if you don't know him. And here's another: To know a person well you must eat a *tomolo*[78] of salt with him. We can more or less say that you have hung around a good bit of time together, and perhaps you've eaten a good deal of salt with him, and you still haven't discovered what kind of person he is. If I had known

---

[76] Usually translated as "outcome" or "result". Derived from *ri-* plus *uscire*, literally "to go out again" and apparently used by Antonio in this literal sense, referring to the procession from the home to the church for a funeral mass. It seems to have been a local term used only in Cerchio.

[77] The punctuation has been corrected here as in other letters. However, it is worth noting that Antonio is aware of the need for such marks.

[78] See Weights and Measures. Roughly two bushels of volume.

him before I wouldn't have given her of blessed memory to him even if he had a million in the post office. But what's done is done and can't be repaired. May Pasquccia be in the glory of Paradise and may they pay for all the evil they have done...

A short undated note, probably late March or April 1911, telling Angelo that Pasquccia's little girl is now being cared for in the nearby town of Aielli.

Dear son,
Your niece Marietta is very well. She is with the wet-nurse in Aielli, who is sending her to school with the nuns. Your mother and your sister went to visit her at Aielli once, and when the weather is good they will go again, but we don't visit with Giovanni. I arranged the mass for the blessed memory of Pasquccia – if you can believe it the girl looks five years old.

Antonio hasn't heard from Angelo in months and is wondering whether he has done something to annoy his son. He has, as we will learn in the next letter, but for now Antonio can only guess that Angelo is annoyed because Antonio's recent letters have been sent by way of Mariuccia's husband Vincenzo, rather than directly. He also suspects that Giovanni, Pasquccia's husband, has been making trouble, which indeed he has. Maria Domenica is going through a bad spell with her edema.

Dear son,   May 1, 1911
I would like to know if there is some reason that you are so slow in writing me and replying to my letters. I got one from you a day after the one you sent to Mariuccia, and since at that very moment I was writing her reply I replied to you also with a few lines at the bottom of her letter, and the letter that Vincenzo wrote to Mariuccia yesterday made me worry a lot. He wrote a letter that didn't say anything about you. The letter I sent you with Vincenzo's address, in which I told you about Pasquccia's death, I addressed to him because I didn't know your box number, and meanwhile you haven't given me any reply.

With this note I inform you that I am in reasonable health, but for about three months your mother has had an illness that doesn't improve. Every day she has sharp pains in the intestines and the belly, and a swollen stomach, and she can't eat at all, and what is worse she doesn't want to have the doctor visit, because he can't cure her, and she can't go to the specialist to get the medicines he prescribes because one must pay in cash. Every now and then she takes a purge, but she doesn't get any relief.

I know that pig Giovanni has written you a letter against us. I would like you to send it to me for my information and out of curiosity. But don't pay any attention to his gossip because everything that he says is false, vile traitor that he is.

In Vincenzo's letter I see that you enjoy good health. We are glad of it. I have many other things to tell you but I'm in haste. Write often, and always reply to my letters...

Angelo finally replies, and Antonio learns that Giovanni has been writing his friend with his version of the story of Pasquccia's death. Antonio angrily rebuts the accusations, and repeats his own version in which Giovanni appears in the worst possible light. Maria Domenica is still ill and Antonio bitterly remarks that the weeds are doing the work of propping up the crops for him. At the end of this letter is the first indication of the strain developing between Mariuccia and her husband Vincenzo (described more fully in Chapter 10).

My dear son,   May 10, 1911

Having just received your long-awaited letter, I reply without wasting a minute to tell you that I see a harsh reproach in which you say that I'm an old man, and that I haven't put aside my feelings. Let me tell you that you grew up with that lying reckless person and you still don't know what he's like. You believe the lies of someone who said that he wanted to write to you but you haven't written to me any more, rather than believing the truth from me. It's true that I made a scene in the church, but what I did wasn't much. I should have done a lot more; the fault was his and not mine. Let's set that aside, because if you want to know about it I've written about it in another letter. Let's get to the *riuscita*. Would you have gone to his house to get him and bring him to the church, and then bring him back home, without having been invited, or even told what day the *riuscita* would be? And not only were we not told, but none of our relatives were told, so how could we go to the house? And who would we be going to console? We'd be consoling those who only two days before said in public before everybody, "The cross should come to the house tomorrow." Write a note to Aunt Domenica and find out from her about what I've said above, and you'll see what she says.

You also said that you don't believe a husband would be so hardhearted to his wife. He was bad enough; she died not only of illness but also of weakness and heartbreak. I say weakness because for more than two months before her death they gave her no more than a nickels-worth of milk, and no more than one glass of wine. I say heartbreak because when she asked him for something she needed, he said "I don't have any money. Get it from your father who should be giving it to you, and then I'll buy it. What's Angelino doing; why hasn't he finished paying the dowry? I've taken on a mule."79 Does this sound to you like a loving husband? His wife dying in bed, his mother went off to take a nap and he went to play Tombola.80 His wife with a priest at the bed and he went off to spade the ground, and when he came back he didn't have the manners to approach us and at least shake our hands, without even shedding a tear. And then he had the nerve to write about us, but he didn't write about what he did. Believe me, he did it. I've renounced him as a son-in-law because he himself said that none of us should call him one because he won't reply.

You reproach me because I asked about Tommaso. I didn't ask for any particular reason, just to find out what he's doing and how he is. I don't know what's going on between the two of you.

---

79 Possibly because a mule is sterile; Pasquccia has turned out to be "sterile" because the dowry has not been paid.

80 Similar to Bingo and possibly the origin of the game. Players have cards with random numbers on them, which are progressively called out from slips drawn from a rotated drum. The name is said to derive from *tombolare*, to tumble.

As to the Notary, I've told you before: I've gone twice and he wasn't there. When I go back I'll find out about the *rinuncia* and also ask him for the copy.

Let's move on to family matters. I'm glad to hear that you're in good health, but I doubt it because the last letter from Vincenzo gave me a certain feeling, and this one today is not like you. My health is fragile, as I keep telling you, and your mother has been seriously ill for about two months, perhaps more. She doesn't stay in bed, she gets up and does some little thing, but the illness will get worse. Her belly is swollen as far as the stomach, and she has constant pains in the intestines. She hasn't gone to see the doctor because she wouldn't be able to take the cures he prescribes because we can't spend a cent, either for medicine or for something to eat because we've been stripped of everything and it's got around that I don't have anything any more. I can't get a loan from anyone, even for a nickel, because they won't give it to me, and so we lead a life that can be compared to that of Isidoro Ninuccio – when he earns a bit of bread he eats it and when he has nothing he fasts. But at least there's no hard work to do; poppies have propped up the fava and grain for me, I can't keep any day-laborers, for about 15 days it's been cold, windy and raining and we can't mow. So here's a second bad harvest coming, worse than the one last year.

I don't want to go on longer because it's long enough, but I've remembered another comment in your letter; you say I'm writing things I shouldn't. Yes, I should write it to you and it's fitting to repeat it in this one to justify my reasons. I wrote you after he spoke of writing against me, so this is a recital that will not be repeated again.

I move on to greet you with your mother and sister, and greet Vincenzo in the same way, and tell him that I went to reprove Mariuccia about the letters, and she replied that since he lets you read her letters, she will also let you see those he has written. She also had me read them and they are very ugly...

Apparently the disagreement has been smoothed over and no more will be said about it. Antonio gives his son a vivid picture of his wife's state of health. Angelo has sent another 200 *lire* and Antonio explains carefully how it has been spent, mostly for agricultural expenses. He has finally found the notary in his office, and learned that Angelo cannot renounce financial responsibility until after his father's death. The crops are filled with weeds and of middling quality. Antonio is still a little nervous that he may offend his son by using Vincenzo's address and makes a point of explaining his reason.

Dear Son,   June 27, 1911

I was very comforted to get your letter on the 16th of this month, in which I learn of your perfect state of health. I'm very glad of it. As for me, I should thank the Lord, considering how I might be, and other than the trouble from that serious fall I had last year I get along very well doing the business of the countryside. It's just that walking is very annoying and it's absolutely impossible to go to the Bacinetto on foot. And now I don't even have the cart because the wheels have finally broken and I must have them rebuilt. It's been fifteen days since I ordered them from a wheelwright[81] in Pescina and we settled on a price of 75 *lire*. He should deliver it to me on July 10 if he keeps his word, since he has 15 *lire* as down payment.

Your sister is in perfect health. As to your mother, her illness is very dangerous, and very very expensive. In addition to the medicine, the doctor has ordered that she must eat chicory fried with lard, onions also fried in lard, as much milk as she can hold, bottled coffee – and each bottle holds something less than two glasses and costs two *lire* and twenty-five centimes – and raw eggs. And this is what she must live on; bread, meat, pasta, and even drinking wine are forbidden. Imagine how she looks now; she's like a piece of wood dried out in the oven but she still has that huge belly that looks as though she were nine months pregnant. There have been two other cases in Cerchio of this illness of water in the body; one was the wife of Felicitto Cicarelli, and the other Rocchitto Proietti, who has returned from America. But they went to the Hospital at Rome and are cured. It's impossible for me to send her to Rome – how would I support her? I'd need at least two or three hundred *lire* to spare – where do I find them?

---

[81] Best available translation of *fagocchio*, a man who fits the iron rim around the wooden cart wheel.

I got the 200 *lire* that you sent. I had to pay a *salma* of grain that I got from the Signora a long time ago, and another half-*salma* I got today: sixty *lire*. I had to pay several day-workers for winnowing the grain and plowing the fava beans and so many other things. In short, I have about twenty *lire* left, and those I gave to your Mother so that she could buy the necessities she must have, because everything that she needs for sustenance must be purchased, even the eggs, because we have six hens but they haven't laid a single egg – and eggs are one and a half *soldi* each. I will do everything that I can, and also try to do more than I can, and then we put our faith in glorious S. Rocco, and hope that he will free her.

But don't think that your Mother stays in bed. No, she gets up and puts on some stitch of clothing, but she barely has the strength to get an onion from the garden and go to mass. You might say she keeps herself on her feet with difficulty because she has been sick for a long time. So I repeat: look to God, and S. Rocco.

In previous letters you spoke several times about the *rinuncia*. Yesterday I went to Pescina expressly to consult with the lawyer about this matter. He told me that a *rinuncia* made before my death is worthless; the *rinuncia* is valid after the death of the person whom one wishes to renounce and here is how you do it:

The person who wants to make the *rinuncia* presents himself to the Clerk of the Magistrate's Court and says to him: "On such-and-such day my Father died. I hereby totally renounce the Paternal [*asso*? assets?],[82] debt, and capital." If you are still in America you can do it with the Consul, and he will send it to the Magistrate's Court. But let's hope that you will all be present at my death. It's very unlikely the Lord will grant me much more time, so when he calls me I must go, and there's nothing to be done about it.

---

[82] Handwriting is cramped, but the word looks like "*asso*". Usual translation is "ace" as in cards. However, the word is so similar to "assets", which itself fits so well in the context that Antonio may be using it as such.

As to the countryside, the grain is reasonably visible but it's not yet ripe, but the [*cordeschi*]83 are of bad quality, the fava all have aphids,84 and the maize and beans are pretty weak and we can't manage to clear them of all the weeds we have this year. Suffice it to say that 20 days went by to plow 5 *coppe* of fava fields in the Bacinetto and I couldn't even finish it. In the end I had to shell them by hand. This year there are poppies sown in the Bacinetto instead of crops...

Agostino is still in Viterbo, he hasn't replied to you because he doesn't have the address. It's been several days since he has asked me for it, so in order not to make a mistake I sent him Vincenzo's. Don't be offended if it isn't addressed to you because I told him to do it this way.

The second case of Antonio attempting to ghostwrite a letter from America in order to manipulate someone in Cerchio. This time it's his wife, to whom Antonio transferred title to his property during his illness. It seems she refuses to pay for repairs to the wagon (*sciarabbà*), so Antonio carefully scripts Angelo's supposed letter, which is also to include directions for the produce.

Dear Son,   July 11, 1911

...Today the reaping began. The daily wages of the reapers cost a great deal, first because for several days a *tramontana* has been reigning so strong that it's indescribable, and it's pretty cold. In the second place every *camparole*85 is hurrying to harvest the grain because on July 4th a thunderstorm totally destroyed Lecce's fields, and partly those of Menaforno and Ortucchio. Let's hope that God will let us escape such a disaster.

Now in this letter I tell you that you must write a letter to your mother, without an envelope. You must make it on a large sheet of paper and enclose it without an envelope like the

---

83 Clearly some sort of crop, but diligent search has failed to turn up any translation. It must be a local dialect term. Antonio also uses the dialect word *mazzocche* when referring to maize; the usual Italian word is *granturco*.

84 Tentative translation of Antonio's *polci* , by analogy with French *poux* = lice.

85 A cooperative group of farmers and their employees formed during harvest time for more efficient reaping and collection of the grain.

one you wrote to Mariuccia last year, and write it precisely as
I've done for you below, and in writing this letter you mustn't
delay even one day, but do it as soon as you get this. You could
also put on it a date three or four days before the day you write
it. Write it as I've done here:

My Dear Mother

It's been a long time since I sent you the money so that
you could buy a draft animal for me, and have the *sciarabbà*[86]
repaired, and you haven't yet let me know anything. You just
told me that you bought a mare. Consequently, if you haven't
yet had the *sciarabà* repaired, I advise you not to lose time to
arrange it for me, because I may be coming back quite soon,
and I don't want to have to work the ground with a spade. I
want to use my ingenuity in other efforts to earn something
for me and you to live on. Also let me know what you've done
about sowing the fields in the Bacinetto. If you have sowed
some fava beans try to find some method and way to get back
about half a *salma* so that you can take good care of the mare
for me, because I am certain that they will make you deposit it
in the warehouse because of the debt with the Administration.
So try to find a way to hide a few of them. But if because of
your illness you can't do it, or you don't know how to settle
with the wheelwright for the best result, so as to see if the work
has been done well or not, then have my father do it, or Uncle
Carmine, but it's always better to have father do it because he's
a bit more competent.

The address: Signora Maria Domenica Meogrossi fù Salvatore, Cerchio

I advise you to write it at once, and without the envelope,
and have it get to me as fast as possible, and be careful not to
make a mistake in the places where I scratched things out to
make corrections...

Disaster strikes; Antonio's produce has been sequestered by
several creditors. Convinced that they are in the wrong, he has tak-
en the matter to court, filing a *reclamo* – a protest and request for

---

[86] Abruzzo dialect for a small wagon with parallel wooden seats, derived from the French
"charabanc".

reconsideration – on behalf of his wife as owner of the contract. Here he descends into the morass of the Italian legal system; the case has been postponed already and it will be almost two years before it is heard. On another matter, he informs Angelo that it will cost 6.5 *lire* to get a copy of Angelo's mortgage document. Moreover, Angelo is late in paying the notary for a previous expense, and his *fondiaria* (property tax bill) has just arrived.

Dear Son,   August 17, 1911
    I reply to your letter that reached me on the eighth of this month. I delayed these few days, first to wait for your other letter written on July 20th, and I received it on the fourteenth of August, (along with the 40 *lire* on that day), all torn and half split open. The second reason for delay has been this: that on July 22nd I received a sequestration order in the Bacinetto from Luigi Fasciani, and another from Francesco Tucceri together with that of Brother-in-law Francesco on August seventh, and they have sequestered all of the grain and [*cordeschi*]. (I hope they'll have to put their hands on their asses and lick them). I have filed the *reclamo*[87] from your mother and today I was supposed to present the case, then it didn't happen and it's been postponed to the 31st of this month, and that's why I delayed, because I wanted to let you know the result. According to the opinion of the lawyer and the employee of the Torlonia Administration in Avezzano to whom I went yesterday – and he issued me the certificate – they will have to pay the expenses. Meanwhile I haven't been able to get back even one *coppa* of produce. Let's hope that Fortune will attend me so that I will make them put a hand to the wall. The fourteenth was a lucky day for me when that forty *lire* arrived, otherwise I wouldn't have had anything to grasp at to pay for the case, and who knows when money will disappear? I have spent thirty *lire* for the *reclamo* and to register the certificate to carry on the case, and it may go to double. Now I have to dance to their tune, but if it's up to me they'll be the ones to dance.
    On the day that I went to file the *reclamo* at Celano I also went to the Notary and found his clerk there. I asked him

---

[87] Literally "complaint", used by Antonio in the legal sense referring to a protest against an action and request for reconsideration.

about the copy and he said there was no point in a copy because the copy of the mortgage contract is valid; if I really wanted it I would have to pay £ 6,50. I told him that the cost of the copy was included in the sum requested, but he said No, and he also told me that you should hurry up with sending the other £ 45. So I told him that you had written that you can't do it now, and that he must have patience once again.

I see from your letter that you enjoy perfect health; we're glad to hear it. As to our health I can't tell you that we're well, nor that we're ill; my health is very frail but I manage to work as long as I don't have to travel on foot. As to your mother she is still in the same condition; her illness doesn't retreat but neither does it advance, her belly is still swollen as before. Mariuccia is well.

The *fondiaria*[88] has come addressed to you and by the tenth day you must pay £ 3.15, half of it.

The case has been postponed, so all the produce remains sequestered in the warehouse. Antonio is so convinced of his rightness that he rejects an offer to settle out of court, taking refuge in the excuse that the land is in his wife's name. He moves on to ask Angelo to try to make an arrangement with two creditors and to raise some money by hook or crook so that they can pay off Carmine d'Alessandro, who holds the mortgage on Angelo's property and is now trying to buy up the family's other IOUs.

My Dear Son,   Sept. 4, 1911
... In my last I told you that the case of your mother's opposition to the sequestration of Fasciani and Tucceri would be heard on the 31st, but it's the nature of the Celano magistrate to postpone hearings and not even have them summoned and so it's been set for October 19th. I'm annoyed about this, because I don't have anywhere to plant the potatoes, and we have nothing to eat and the fava, the grain, the beans and the potatoes are in the hands of the Receiver. But it doesn't matter, time will pass, money may go, but a day will come when they

---

[88] Usually used to refer to a large area of land roughly equivalent to the English "plantation", but Antonio uses it to mean the rent paid for the land.

will pay everything, because everything that's been done is valid and we can't possibly be in the wrong. Just today Fasciani asked me if I'd be willing to make an arrangement without going to court. I told him that he should see about it with your mother because I wasn't part of this case and that he should repay the expenses we've made and I will give him a little at a time when I can for what I owe him, and without interest. We'll see what he says.

Now let me tell you that I want you to write a letter to Francesco Perille, begging him to be content with just the interest this year, and the same to Pietro d'Alessandro of Coll'Armele,89 and also try to find some way, even if you have to get a loan, to hang Carmine d'Alessandro by the balls, because aside from the fact that he's going around boasting that he's got a foot in the door and that in a short while it will all be his, he's also trying to buy up the IOUs of others. So if you can make this payment it will be a celebration, and also because the interest is very expensive. I've discussed it with him because the tax collector has made him pay a registration tax of 70 *lire* in addition to what he paid the Notary, and I didn't want to acknowledge it. He said that he will do it through the courts, but so far he hasn't done anything, so try to do it if you can...

Cholera has struck, and Antonio describes the situation in the town. Several of their relatives have died, although the quarantine is so strict that the hospital isn't giving out information. The pope has banned public celebration of most holy days, earning Antonio's disgust. Angelo has sent another 430 *lire*, with instructions to pay off two creditors but Antonio argues that it is more important to erase the debt with d'Alessandro, who is becoming very threatening. The case drags on, costing money each time it is put on the docket, even though it doesn't get heard.

---

89 Modern spelling of the town is the single word Collarmele, and Antonio usually writes it that way. His writing here is probably an archaic version. According to the web site www.collarmele.terremarsicane.it, one Andrea di Pietro believes that the town is derived from the union of several smaller villages, including Colle and Armele.

Dear son,   Sept. 27, 1911

I got your letter dated the sixth of this month in which I see that you enjoy the best of health. I am extremely glad to hear it. We by the grace of God are reasonably well; I'm holding up pretty well except for some shortness of breath, and your mother's illness seems to have diminished a bit, but we think we're alive and yet don't believe it, because there's been a very ugly cholera in Cerchio that had terrified the whole country although it lasted a short while, for in fifteen days about twenty have died and we still don't know with certainty the number and who they are, because the Hospital has closed and they don't say who it is or isn't when someone dies. For about twenty days we have had two municipal guards from L'Aquila,90 a doctor, male nurse, and four people from the Red Cross, and they have worked hard in these days to disinfect all the buildings of Cerchio. It's now been about ten days that we haven't heard of any other case of illness. Let's hope our patron saint San Rocco will take away this infectious evil and deliver us. After these sicknesses the festivals have been prohibited by the prefect, then the Pope has completely banned all feasts, both secular as well as religious. He has only kept for feast days all Sundays, Christmas, New Years, Easter, Epiphany and Ascension. All other days are days of work; he hasn't kept the day of Corpus Domini as a feast day, nor even the day of the Nativity of the Madonna, September eighth. (In my opinion this Pope must be a member of the most protestant groups. He does as he pleases.)

Now I move on to tell you that in your letter you told me that I should have paid Perille and Pizitto with the 430 *lire* you sent. It seems to me that in a note included with a letter to Vincenzo I indicated that my opinion would be to hang Carmine d'Alessandro of Collarmele by his boots and get back what we tied up with him two years ago, because he's been spreading a lot of rumors saying that he wants to buy up other IOUs of mine and join them to the mortgage he has, and he wants to do this because we're having quite a disagreement because I don't want to recognize seventy *lire* more that the tax collector made him pay for surtax. And so I would be of this opinion. If you are also of this opinion reply to me at once by

---

90 The provincial capital

post so that your reply gets to me in time for the end of October. Don't delay as you usually do.

The hearing for the *reclamo* that your mother is making against Luigi Fasciani and Francesco Tucceri was rescheduled by the Magistrate for the nineteenth of October. Meanwhile my hands are tied, without my being able to recover even a potato, and what is worse, within a few days I'm going to dig up the potatoes and I must find to place for rent to deposit them, because I can't put them in the Torlonia warehouse because it's full of grain. I hope that in the end it will cost them a lot "although they're giving me a lot of leeway", and a big expense of money and gifts for the lawyers. Enough, it doesn't matter, as long as the result is favorable for me. According to the lawyer's opinion it should not go against me.

...I advise you to write to Agostino and send him some money because I can't send him even a cent. His address is:

Sig. Augusto Vasquenz, Prisoner in the Viterbo Prison, Province of Rome

P.S. Those of our relatives who have died are Graziuccia, and Mariuccia di Nerone, and possibly the daughters of Aunt Domenica di Genova.

Angelo insists on paying the other creditors first, and so Antonio dutifully reports the results. Aside from partial payments to several creditors he's also had to pay for seed grain, plus a fee for the sequestered produce, some of which he is allowed to buy back. There was also a hefty fee to file the *reclamo*. At this point, Antonio begins to feel that he has invested so much in the case that he will lose money if he withdraws it, with the result that he will spend a lot more in future.

My dear son,   Nov. 4, 1911
I'm replying to your letter although I delayed a few days to wait for your other one to find out if you agreed with my thoughts, but now that I've learned that you prefer to get rid of

the other raging Corsicans[91] I have spent the money as explained here: I paid off the IOU to Davide Ciaglia of Collarmele in full because he was the most enraged. I've given half to Perille; for the remaining half he wants another IOU because he didn't want to give me a receipt. I'm sending it to you in this letter; you sign it and send it back and then we'll get back the old one. I only gave six *lire* to Pietro d'Alessandro for the interest on the thirty *lire*, and I gave Carmine d'Alessandro the interest for two years for the IOU of thirty *lire*, because I didn't give him anything last year. I've sent thirty *lire* to the man at San Pelino but haven't received a reply yet. I gave Pizitto the value of one *salma* of grain at thirty-six *lire*. I still have to give him six *coppe* of grain and to get back two *salme* of grain for sowing. Since the case still isn't decided I had to sign over seventy *lire* to the Depositor, and another seventy *lire* to get back a few potatoes and half a *salma* of maize, and I had to deposit one hundred *lire* to file the *reclamo* to the sequestration, which in total amounts to £552.50. That's twenty-two *lire* more than you sent. There are the 25 *lire* that were deposited with Francesco Rametti last year. The money that I've spent for the sequestration will all be refunded at the end of the case because there's good hope that we will win it, but it could be in their favor for all my efforts. The lawyer tells me that they can't possibly be right; we shall see.

In your letter you said that I should have paid the notary. I haven't been able to pay him so far because I had to protect myself as I said above. On the eighteenth when I go back to Celano to hear the witnesses I will go see him and tell him he must be patient again and explain the situation. If you had told me before I wouldn't have paid Davide Ciaglia everything. Thirty-seven *lire* have already gone for the two hearings so far, and the *reclamo*, the lawyer and the court fees, aside from the presents and that's the forty *lire* that you sent your Mother. This hearing on the 18th makes me think, because it costs a lot more for the witnesses whom I ought to pay. I include for you this note with the full account so don't get angry to find it in this letter. When you reply to this and send back the IOU that

---

[91] Most accurate translation of Antonio's *corsi*. If he did intend "Corsicans", he was probably using a national stereotype, since Corsicans were frequently thought of as savage uncivilized bandits, outlaws and highwaymen. In another letter he refers to one creditor as an assassin.

I'm sending, I will get back the IOU from Perille and send it to you, as well as that of Ciaglia.

The things I recovered in the Bacinetto are all deposited with the Receiver, and that would be seven and a half *salme* of grain because I got back two for sowing, two *salme* of fava beans and two *salme* of maize, and three *coppe* of beans, and five *coppe* of land for beets, and so far nothing has come into the house, only what I told you above that I renegotiated with the hundred and forty *lire* that I had to pay to the Receiver. I can't tell you any more about this for now until I learn the decision of the case...

Maria Domenica has a touch of pneumonia, and Antonio carefully describes the treatment recommended by the doctor. Feeling her age, and recognizing her legal ownership of Antonio's assets, she wants to make a will in favor of Angelo and the imprisoned Agostino, pointedly ignoring the delinquent Tommaso who never writes or sends money. Agostino seems to have gotten married before his imprisonment, so the problem is how to leave the money to him without the wife getting hold of it. There is no indication what crime Agostino committed, but even the loyal Antonio admits that he is guilty. Apparently Angelo is very concerned to get copies of all documents, and Antonio explains why he can't always comply. The case drags on.

Dear Son,   January 1, 1912
...By the grace of God I am reasonably well, as is your sister Mariuccia. But for your mother – in all the other letters I've always said that we all enjoy perfect health, but it's rather that your mother had gotten much better from that sickness she had. But for about ten days now she has been like one slightly convalescent, with small pains in her waist and a little bit of fever. Sometimes she was hot and sometimes cold. Until today she didn't want to have the doctor called. This morning I was forced to have him visit and he found that she has an infection in the lungs. We hope this will be a minor matter, because the doctor said that if we use the greatest possible attention he hopes she will get well quickly. The attention we must use is this: the first thing is to protect her from cold, keep the doors

and windows closed. At least a liter of milk a day, three or four good coffees, broth, and as many eggs as she can suck, in addition to the medicine. I will make any sacrifice and try to do even more than the doctor ordered and hope the Lord will watch over the family's needs and grant us a quick cure.

Now I must tell you that for several days she's been asking me to take her to the notary to make a will of her liquid assets,92 and she wants to name you and Agostino, because if the poor fellow isn't remembered he'll be left bare, without even a family tie. While he has committed that error, it could happen to anyone. Also, as a scruple of conscience he should be remembered as a son – not from my property, because I've been stripped of everything, but at least from what little your mother possesses. But the problem is that he can't sign the will because of the Fusara woman and the legal expenses, so we must figure out how to do it.

I got a letter from Agostino a few days ago and he told me he got the 35 *lire* and that I should thank you for him, and he also told me that on November 19 the prison director had granted him permission to be able to write you, and he certainly will have done so.

As to the IOU above the amount I beg you not to worry about it because Perille has renewed it, since there were no other bills. £147.15 is left from the 261.65 *lire*, as was written on the back. I'm sending you the IOU of Davide Ciaglia of Collarmele. Clarice's IOU was canceled when I returned the 57 *lire* to her. If that doesn't reassure you, I'll send you a note from Giovannino [Clarice's husband] in another letter and you'll feel more certain. But I can't send you the obligation of Pizitto because he didn't want to return it to me because I still have to give him another six *coppe* of grain. I wanted him to make a new one but he wouldn't.

As to the case, the lawyer tells me we can't lose. On January 20th I must bring the evidence, and I will bring Don Lorenzo Sperra and Nicolino Cavasinni,93 but the problem is that it's getting to be a sack of money. The case is running very long and I haven't been able to bring home even a potato from

---

92 *Disponibile* = available or disposible goods

93 We know from other letters than Don Sperra is the local representative of the Torlonia Administration. Antonio clearly has the authorities on his side.

the Bacinetto, it's all been sold without my being able to get even a nickel, everything that was withdrawn all had to be put in the Post Office.

I got the 100 *lire* yesterday and went at once to pay the notary with 45 *lire*. He told me that the copy of the deed wasn't included, if I wanted it I would have to pay, but there was no need because there is the copy of the mortgage...

The will has been held up over several concerns, but we will see in the next letter that it did get written. The case drags on, costing more and more money, but Antonio just gets more stubborn with each postponement. On a revealing side note, there are no stamps available in Cerchio.

My Dear Son,   Feb. 5, 1912
...your mother still isn't back to perfect health after the illness she had that I wrote to you about in my last letter, because the pains in her stomach and viscera never stop. But we thank God, because after what happened I thought I wouldn't have her any more. Let's hope he will bring her back to perfect health, but it's very unlikely she will regain the health of before.

As to the decision your mother made to recognize you and Agostino from her liquid assets, it's very unlikely she can do it, in the first place because the government won't allow it, and in the second place it will cost a lot. But when I go to Celano on Saturday to bring the evidence for the hearing I will consult with the lawyer and see if we can come to an agreement, but then perhaps he will see some difficulty. Do you think we want to spend money and then redo a project that will cost who knows how much? But with regard to this you can be sure that what she does will be done forever.

As to the case, that pig of a magistrate at Celano has been stretching it out so much that I'm sick and tired of going to Celano so many times, and shelling out so much money and gifts. The first hearing was supposed to be August 31, it was postponed to October 19, the opposing lawyer called for evidence to testify if the sequestration had been done solely on

land your mother owns,94 and this hearing was set for November 18, from November 18 it was postponed to January 20,
and from January 20 to February 10. When we get to that day
we'll see how it comes out, and when he will pass sentence.
Meanwhile it's been three times that I've brought witnesses
and shelled out money to pay them and subpoena them. But I
repeat I hope for a good result according to what the lawyer as-
sures me, and I hope the only benefit they get is the trouble
they've given me for all my efforts. The lawyer tells me they
can't do anything to me; let's hope that's true, as I also hope
the sentence will hurry up because I am pretty badly entangled.
I haven't turned over even a nickel to the Administration, and
I have nothing for the family because it was all sold and the
money put in the Post Office at Celano. So it was really a lucky
chance that you sent those 100 *lire* because if you hadn't sent
them I would have had to get in debt to provide for the trial if
necessary, and everything else.

Daviduccio is in America again, he's with Giovanni and
Rico.95 But tell me why you're making this inquiry; we're imagining some strange event.

So far we haven't seen any snow, just a little in the mountains, and there was a little on the plain on Jan. 16, but the next
day a *tramontana* and then a little *scirocco* destroyed it in a
moment, and today it's rained buckets all night...

P.S. Several days ago your sister wrote to her husband Vincenzo, and because there aren't any stamps in Cerchio she had to
reopen it and put it with the one to you. So tell her husband
not to get annoyed this time if we made it all one letter.

Also, let me know if you got the insured letter with the
IOUs from Perille and Davide Ciaglia of Collarmele, and the
letter from Agostino was also included to reassure you that he
did reply. Answer quickly.

---

94 We never learn clearly why Antonio is so sure he will win the case, but this may be a
hint: If the debt was that of Antonio, then land and produce now belonging to his wife is
perhaps exempt from the sequestration.

95 Davide and Giovanni Meogrossi, Angelo's cousins on his mother's side, were in Nottingham, Ohio, at the time. Rico is probably Enrico Vasquenz, who was in Cleveland.

As the case drags on, a new problem arises: unable to access the produce Antonio cannot pay his annual rent to the Torlonia Administration, of which Signor Sperra is the representative. Sperra professes that his hands are tied and advises Antonio to pay the rent lest he lose the contract, so Antonio begs Angelo to come up with the funds. To sweeten the pill, he promises that Maria Domenica will transfer title jointly to Angelo and Agostino, who can then work out how to share it. Almost as an afterthought, Antonio mentions that the will has been written.

Dear Son,   March 17, 1912
    Annoyed because I have been deprived of your news for a long time, I come to send this off to you and let you know that by the grace of God we enjoy reasonable health, although not perfect, but we thank the Lord that he may keep us always thus....

    Now I move on to inform you about the case. A magistrate is a very nasty animal, and so the one who holds the Magistrate's Court in Celano is an animal, because he has been stretching out the case so much that it will not end during my lifetime. It's been four times now that I've brought the evidence, and he has never held a hearing, always putting it off for a long time. Yesterday I had to bring it back yet again; there wasn't even a hearing and he wanted to reschedule it for the middle of July. After many pleas from the lawyer, with much difficulty, he settled for rescheduling it for May 30, after the lawyer had promised that we are sure of having a favorable sentence. But the time is long, and everything that I'd produced is deposited with the Receiver without my being able to get back even a nickel until the case is decided. It's not so much the thought of the family's needs, because we try to do the best we can; my big grudge is that I haven't been able to give anything to the Administration. I spoke with Signor Sperra to try to get him to file a *reclamo* for the property. He replied that the Administration doesn't make *reclami* for sums less than eight hundred *lire*, and he also told me that I should try to find a way to pay at least the yearly fee, because if I delay any more I could lose the lands. So with this I want to beg you, if it's possible (although I'm ashamed to say it to you, but necessity compels me) if you can, even at the cost of getting a loan, you must send me three hundred and ten *lire* to pay at least the basic annual fee. And when you pay over this sum your mother has decided to put the lands in your name and Agostino's and then when it's settled you can agree between the two of you how to avoid what he would have to give to the Fusara. So if you can, don't fail to do this because, I repeat, I'm afraid of losing the lands, and then what will we have to live on? And you should send it to me by telegram as soon as you get this, and I advise you not to be so slow in writing as you have been, because we are imagining a thousand things; we have no way of knowing what may have happened to you.

On the 14th I got a letter from Agostino. He's in good health. He would like a bit of money, but I can't do it. Although he has never asked me for it, I can tell by the way he writes. He just asked me many times for an instructive book, and one on arithmetic, and I couldn't even send him that through helplessness. In his letter he complains that he's written you two letters and still hasn't received any reply. I beg you not to abandon him, at least write often.

PS: I forgot to tell you that your mother made the will on February 10th. I haven't had a copy made yet because I have to pay another 13 *lire*.

Tommaso and Angelo are getting along now, although that will change when Tommaso learns about the will. Apparently Antonio doesn't even know where Tommaso is living, since he never writes.

My dear son,   March 24, 1912

I reply to your letter dated March 5, in which I see that you as well as your brother Tommaso enjoy perfect health. I am extremely glad, as I am glad to hear that you have made peace, but you've never told me how the problem arose between you. With this I must express my complaints of you because you are somewhat dilatory in writing. Annoyed by this delay I wrote you a letter on March 17 and in that I told you all about the case. I repeat it here: we hope for a good outcome, but I'm drying the beans and I'm fed up with making trips to Celano because it's been postponed many times. I've taken it to court four times and they cost a fair amount. Now it's been rescheduled for May 30. Let's hope that on that day Mr. Magistrate kicks the bucket in deciding it.

I would have replied sooner but on the evening of the 19th (San Giuseppe's Day) your mother was assailed again by a bad colic. I pass over her sufferings; sufficient to say I had to take care of her all night. Now she's in reasonable health. I can't say she's well, but then I can't say she's ill. The visceral pains never stop; it's impossible that she will regain her former health.

In the letter of the 17th I asked you to send something if you can to pay the Administration. Don't fail to do it even if it means getting a loan because we run the risk of losing the fields. If you can, do it as soon as possible. Let me know if you got the insured letter containing the IOUs of Perille and Davide Ciaglia. I beg you not to delay in writing as you have done in the past.

In your reply to this let me know if you're with Tommaso, or if you're apart. Try to keep the peace, and also let me know how his health is, if the illness has struck him again or whether he's cured, and how he's doing financially. Then thank him on my behalf, because he hasn't had the courtesy to write me even a line of paper since he left Cerchio. But it's enough if he's well, he and Rosa. In Cerchio they were saying that she's pregnant; let me know if it's true.

We didn't see any snow around here at all this winter, but now there's been about eight days of constant rain on the plain and snow in the mountains. There've been several frosts, and I sent the almond flowers for the Blessing in Roma, but I'm pretty unhappy about the two plum trees in the garden, and today there's a strong *tramontana* blowing so that one can't work in the countryside. Let's hope it won't damage the grain because it's full of weeds, so that this year we have to recover it by winnowing because there's a lot of grass, poppies and alfalfa.

I won't go on any more because I have to go to the Bacinetto tomorrow to take the potatoes for planting...

Angelo seems to have reached breaking point, despairing that the debts will ever be paid off. Antonio adopts a conciliatory tone, praising Angelo's hard work and pleading that they have no other option and are trying to economize, living on potatoes, eggs and water. He even suggests that Angelo decrease the small amounts sent for discretionary purposes.

Dear Son,   April 15, 1912

I reply with the greatest promptness to your letter in which I see that you all enjoy perfect health...I also note your complaints – we might even say your reproof – because of all the money you have sent back and you still haven't been able remove half the debts that you signed by IOU. Dear son, you are very right, and the money you have been sending back is truly more than I would have believed, but what do you want? In other letters I've made you aware of the whole situation of our family, I have told you that I couldn't bring back even one potato from the Bacinetto, I had to sell everything and the money is all deposited in the Post Office at Celano. I recovered about three *coppe* of beans and didn't want to sell them, with the hope of bringing them home. But that was not granted me by the consignee and he is keeping them as a deposit. So as not to be deprived of food I brought back the rejected potatoes – and I had to pay four *lire* per quintal for them – and two *salme* of grain to sow and for them I had to pay thirty-five *lire* per *salma*. And to pay some little family debt, reaping, plowing, sowing, and so many other things, aside from a little expense for us – certainly it came from your toil, I can't deny it, but don't think that we're spendthrifts for our food. No, we eat potatoes, and pizza without water, just all stuffed up with eggs, and we taste wine when someone comes to make arrangements about the plowing. I assure you that for all the festivals that have come, full bottles have never come into the house.

It's been some days since I received the £180. I'm very obliged to you for them, and with them I've been able to make some profit after having paid for the team to sow the [*cordeschi*] in the Bacinetto and after having bought myself some half *salma* of grain and maize. But Fortune grants me nothing favorable. I've already spent 55 *lire* to keep the women in the Bacinetto to winnow the grain and they haven't yet done half a *salma*; imagine how much it will be to finish winnowing all of it. And what is worse is the bad weather; what it didn't do in past months it's been doing in April. The 4th, 5th and 11th were three strong frosts that took off all the fruits. The 13th, 14th and today the 15th I tell you that no one has been able to

97

drive out the animals to water because of the strong *tramontana* with a dusting of snow, and pretty cold. Suffice it to say that the train had to have the snowplow in front, and so the labors were delayed, the day-workers came back up, and who knows what the end will be for the crops.

I wrote you to have money to pay the Administration precisely so as not to delay another year because the case was rescheduled for May 30, and who knows if it will be decided that day. And I had thought of all this for fear of being thrown off the land. But if you can't do it, I'll have to await perforce the decision of the case.

I wrote you to remember Agostino some time, but I didn't tell you to send us 15 or 20 *lire*. If you want to do us a kindness some time you could send 4 or 5 *lire*, but not as much as you have done in the past. Now my strongest thought is that in October of this year we absolutely must think of paying off the mortgage contract with Carmine d'Alessandro – it doesn't matter if you aren't here, because it can be done without you – and also the thought of the Administration...

The magistrate outdoes himself by adjourning the court without hearing a single case. Angelo still wants copies of documents, and the notary says it is either pointless or impossible. Pasquccia's little daughter Marietta visits her grandparents, and Angelo has kindly sent a little money for her, although Antonio admits he had to appropriate it. The feud with her father Giovanni continues.

Dear Son,   June 6, 1912

I reply to your letter with a delay of about fifteen days in order to wait for the outcome of the case, which was supposed to be heard on May 30, and let you know about it. But since the town of Celano has a magistrate who never brings any case to an end, there were 35 cases to hear on that day at the magistrate's court, but he didn't hear any of them; they were all postponed. Our case was rescheduled for September 12. Given that the case has brought me to such lengths, I had to subpoena the consignee to have him make a judicial deposit of the sums he's holding.

On the same day I went to pay the notary and I asked him for a copy of the title to the house as well as a copy of the will.

He told me that the copy of the title was of no use, because a copy of the mortgage deed is what is needed, and so it was pointless to spend six or seven *lire* for it. And he can't release a copy of the will until it's been registered, and wills are registered after the death. I asked him for it as a favor because I had to send it to you. He replied like this, "Write to your son, and if he doesn't believe you he can write to me, and I will write the same thing to him." So if you want to be more certain, write a note addressed to: Sig. Don Nino Paolini, Notary, Celano." Note that in the letter you should give the date the will was made, so that he can find it immediately. The will was made on February 10, not March 10.

I got the 300 *lire*, but I haven't delivered it yet because I haven't had time. We are burdened with work. Your mother and I can't even manage to gather the hay at Fucino. We're so tired that in the evening we can barely get to bed. I would have handed it over to the Guardia, but since your mother wants to put the lands in your name and Agostino's I have to go to Avezzano, and she must come with me. As soon as I've got through these activities we'll go at once.

... In your reply, let me know how Tommaso is doing, if you are together, and if it's true that Rosa has a son.

The harvest should look good, but it's doubtful because the weather is very bad. Some days the sun scorches you and other days there are evening frosts, and the shoots are pale and ugly. The beans and potatoes and various areas have frozen. Let's hope the Lord will not flay us with some awful disaster.

In your letter you said you were sending 5 *lire* to make a dress for our granddaughter Marietta. I haven't given it to her yet, and I certainly won't hand it over to her father. I'll do better for the June festivals and will buy her either a dress or a pair of shoes, because I needed the 5 *lire* and I took them. As soon as I can scrape them together I'll get what she needs. She's in very good health. She always comes to the house when your mother is home, and for festivals, and Mother and I are pleased with that. But we have nothing to do with her father.

A bad drought has struck, and prospects for the harvest are poor. We note that Antonio does use fertilizers. He plans to use the most recent money from Angelo to pay the town tax and the tax on the fields. Antonio has spotted a house for sale that would be good

for Mariuccia and her husband Vincenzo, and he asks if Angelo has any idea of Vincenzo's financial situation.

My Dear Son,   August 15, 1912

It's 15 days since I received your letter. I've delayed a reply through lack of time.... By God's grace we are in reasonably good health. Let's hope the Lord will keep us free of harm, but this year the air is very subject to outbreaks of infectious sicknesses because of the overwhelming drought that's going on. The little sprinkles we had at the beginning of the harvest were like a fire throughout the countryside. Now the whole world is dried out; the maize, the potatoes and the beans are all dried up without filling out, the fava beans haven't even come up to three,96 and the grain in the fields no more than two and a half, four at the most. In Fucino anyone who could harvest it did, and was lucky that it didn't fall to the ground. I harvested up to ten, and what fell to the ground was no more than six. We can't complain about the grain in Fucino this year, and since the cost for winnowing is pretty small I could recover it. But still I've spent a lot on the winnowing alone without my day-workers, and I had to pay £113 for your Mother aside from the £35 for nitrate. If I hadn't spent all this I wouldn't have reaped a single ear of grain.

I got the £100. I still have them without using them at all; they will go to pay for the winnowing and the current year's fee to the Comune and the *fondiaria*. So we try to stay healthy and turn to the old proverb that says, "What the year brings, the year consumes". But things go at a pretty high price, the best new grain is up to 45 *lire*, fava to 36, and that's at the beginning of the harvest. You can imagine how much it may have gone up since May.

The case was set for September 12. Let's hope it will happen, and I still hope to have a good outcome.

Within a few days I expect a letter from Agostino and then I'll write him what you told me, but I think he will have received it. As for so many other things, you can be very sure of what we've said previously. Without telling Vincenzo let me know how he stands financially, because he doesn't send back

---

96 He doesn't specify the units; in the later sentences it must be volume such as *coppe* or *salme*.

much money, and also let us know if he intends to buy a house when he returns. He can't get one for less than 2000 *lire*. A house of Antonio Chicarelli's turned up near the washing basin,97 which I would like, and it's in a good position, but there are simple walls and roof, and one should raise another half-level above, and he doesn't want to let it go for less than 2000 *lire*, so he will want to know if he has some little bit of money, aside from what he has at the Post Office in Cerchio...

Antonio writes in haste to ask Angelo to send money to pay off the mortgage before the contract year expires, so that they can avoid expenses associated with renewing it. A different creditor might agree to extend his loan another year and accept only the interest for now. The drought has been succeeded by a cold spell, delaying ripening and leaving them with only potatoes to eat.

Dear Son,   Sept. 27, 1912
    Just as I was leaving the house to go to the Bacinetto I received your letter dated the 10th of this month...I've turned back from the trip I'd begun to the Bacinetto to reply to you at once, there being something of great importance, because if I pay off the mortgage for the stable as shown in the contract made in Collarmele, then he won't get any more money and will have to wait another year. Therefore this repayment should be made before the fifteenth of November because on the contract made in Collarmele the date is November 20, 1909. Consequently, if you can make the effort the money should come by post around the end of October, and for this reason I have hastened to reply to your letter. The sum of £470 is needed to make this repayment, then the expenses of the Registrar, and to recover the mortgage registration fees and the notary's indemnity. If you can do all this it should be done promptly and not wait till the expiration date. Of course the repayment will be made in your name. If it turns out it can't be done in your absence I will write at once and then you can send a proxy, so I want you to be prompt. I expected this letter on the 15th, but instead it came today with 12 days delay, so as soon as you receive this one don't lose even one day and don't

---

97 *sciacquatoio* = trough where the laundry is rinsed

drag out doing your duty. And it seems to me that I wrote you about this last year, that I wanted to get rid of this unfinished business. Meanwhile, write a letter to Francesco Perille, saying that if he'll be content with the interest for this year, then next year if we are well it will be resolved. I still hope to give him the interest if the case works out favorably for me, but who knows when he will decide. Now it's been rescheduled for the seventh of November. Let's hope he'll hear it. It would be enough if he doesn't postpone it another time. Reply at once without losing any time.

Now you want to know if I paid the £300 to the Administration. I certainly wouldn't have asked you for it if I didn't want to pay it. So far, aside from that £300 I have paid another £260 in grain, but now the house is cleaned out. We haven't even tried the beans, the chickpeas and the maize because the 14th, 15th and 16th of August there was an intense cold and things like that weren't fully ripe and so we were left with those miserable potatoes and nothing else. If I hadn't committed the maize leaves and the bean twigs to the man who came for the sowing I would have sold the maize left on the ground to get food for the animals as so many others have done, at the valuation of eleven thousand for two *lire* per *coppa*. But we must be patient, I'm getting used to suffering. I spent last year without recovering anything because it was all confiscated by the men of the world. But this year will pass, taken from me by the Father Eternal. Patience I say again, because God has done these things, but if one must pay the damages then Paradise would not be enough even if there were someone who wanted to buy it.

Granddaughter Marietta sends greetings, she stays with us every day. She's looking forward to your return when you bring back the scarf. You had me write to Tommaso but he doesn't reply...

The mortgage to Carmine d'Alessandro has been paid off, with Angelo's uncle acting as his proxy, but when the numerous fees are included Antonio discovers to his rage that there is still a balance owing, so that he had to incur another debt. Pasquccia's widower Giovanni has taken up with another woman, who is rumored to be pregnant, and Mariuccia's troubles with her in-laws are reaching boiling point.

My dear son,   Nov. 15, 1912
        I got your letter on the 12th of November. Yesterday I went to find out if it's possible to redeem Carmine d'Alessandro's deed without your being present. I was told that everything could be done, but a third person must redeem it in your name, and so today I went to Pescina to the notary Mascioli with your uncle Carmine, who redeemed it free and clear in your name and on your behalf, believing me that it wouldn't cost much to make this redemption, as the notary in Celano had told me when I went to him to get this information. But the fact was that I couldn't go to him, and Mascioli hit me up for the principal and everything else so that I had to give that assassin of Collarmele five hundred and nine *lire*, for which I give you the full accounting below, and this sum has been recorded in the deed, and 113 *lire* registration fee and everything else, just as in the detailed record that I'm including with this letter. So I've spent six hundred and twenty-five *lire* total; your uncle Carmine and I had to sign an IOU to the notary for the twenty-five *lire* with a due-date of December 15, next month. Here is the account in detail:

Principal amount according to the deed	£ 400
For the IOU	30
Four years' restoration of the produce, because he already paid for 1913	16
Supplement to the tax collector	<u>66</u>
Here is the sum pocketed by d'Alessandro	512
Then fee for the deed, which costs	<u>£ 113</u>
Total	625

I'm sure you'll shake all over when you read this account, and I can assure you it's seven in the evening and I still haven't been able to eat. I broke out in a fever with rage, because I thought that something would be left for me, but instead I'm still in debt. Still, we have gotten out from under that person who was boasting around Cerchio that by the end of another year this alley will be all his. And if I end up a beggar I don't care at all. He will give me the copy of the deed and of the mortgage when I bring him the 25 *lire*. Answer at once, and let me know if I should send the copy to you, or whether you want me to keep it. I have many other things to tell you but I can't keep my head straight.

Let me know about Tommaso and how he's doing. Tell him to write me a letter; he hasn't had the courtesy to answer me. Your brother-in-law Giovanni has paired up again with Maria Agostina Maccallini (the wife of Giovanni Angelone), but without getting married, and she's prematurely pregnant. We don't know if he's the one, or someone else, but it's more than certain.

I'm glad that you and Vincenzo are well; we are reasonably well. We've been besieged by bad weather; as of today we've had two big snowstorms, and rain with a very strong *tramontana*.

Now I must speak to you on behalf of your sister. She is somewhat indiscreet with her husband. He barely treats her as a wife any more, and so her reply to his letters is a bit exaggerated, but with good reason. Don't let him know anything about what I've said, but try to ascertain his intentions, because when he comes back he will want to go back to his father's house, but Mariuccia doesn't go to that house at all. On the contrary, she's glad to be away from him and not with that household. Let me know about him in secret. He wrote that I should have given him ten *coppe* of land in Fucino and if I didn't give it when he returns he will be like a dog. See what a nice judgment he shows?

I won't go on any more. I just beg you not to get upset about the money spent this time. Try to stay healthy and all will be regained; we have raised a weight from our shoulders. We're left with nothing, but God will provide...

Paperwork from the canceled mortgage is taking a while to process, and Angelo has questioned why the total cost is so high. Antonio doesn't understand it either, although he makes an attempt to explain. Like so many people confronted by real estate finance, he gives up in defeat and just follows instructions. The case, needless to say, still drags on. Tommaso has gotten word about the will, spoiling his relations with Angelo again.

Dear son,   Nov. 25, 1912

I'm answering your letter that reached me on Nov. 16. I've delayed answering a few days to wait for the copy from the notary, which should come back from Aquila. Yesterday I went back and it wasn't even ready. But he must release the copy of the document to me and he couldn't release it because the collector still has it. It will be another ten days or so to get both of them. As soon as I can get it I will immediately write a certified letter and get it off to you.

You may say that it's too much to spend so much money for this action. We can't understand anything about these matters, everything is done their way. I asked him if the copy was included in the sum of 113. He said Yes, and now he wants another six *lire* and forty-five centimes to release the copy, because yesterday he told me that only the copy of the registration was included, and not that of the document. And so we must pay what they say. You told me that when this deed was made with d'Alessandro only 50 *lire* were paid, but you don't know that the tax collector made a supplement of another 85 *lire* which I didn't know anything about. So they've enrolled a government expert, and to avoid this expense d'Alessandro went to make an arrangement with the tax collector and they agreed on another 66 *lire*, and I must pay that back to the person named in the deed of repurchase.

So it's better not to speak about this any more, because I can feel the fever of rage flowing in my veins again. We've hung him by the balls and what he's gained from his sin I pray God he'll spend for a lot of holy oil.

You also say that when the document was made between the two of us 78.98 was spent. Don't you remember the supplement made by the collector of Avezzano? Then add what we paid to the notary and what we paid the collector and you'll see what it adds up to. Everything we've done is all according to prescribed rules.

The case with Luigi Fasciani has not been heard yet. It was supposed to be heard on November 7; the magistrate was out and it didn't happen. I wrote the lawyer; he told me that the officer has rescheduled it for the fourth Monday in January 1913. Let's hope Mr. Magistrate will do it this time, but who knows when he will decide it?

I got a letter from Agostino which mentioned the *lire* you sent him recently. He asked me to give you thanks on his behalf when I write you, and also to Ciccuccio Flaminia, or rather Villanuccio, and he put a note in the letter to me so that I could send it to you because he doesn't have permission to write you, and I sent you this note in a letter that Maria Giuseppa Scampone sent you. When you write back, let me know what the problem is between you and Tommaso. If he's annoyed about what we've done then he doesn't wish us well because if we hadn't done this, then it would be neither his, nor yours, and not even mine from the time they would have expropriated everything, and then perhaps he would be glad about it, that's for sure. But try to avoid chances to quarrel and take care not to make problems between you...

The case drags on, costs mount up and sessions are not even held. A creditor who has been very patient has finally demanded payment. Antonio has had a shot at requesting something like parole or house arrest for Agostino, figuring he has nothing to lose but the cost of the paper.

Dear Son,   January 29, 1913
Just today I got your letter in which I note your perfect state of health. We too are well by the grace of God. As to the problem between you and Tommaso I had already thought of it. He would be justified in complaining in this way if he had supported the family, or if there hadn't been any debts and he hadn't thought about the family at all. Nor would I have taken the responsibility; he would have been treated the same as you. But the storm was looking ugly and I was about to fall on my back, and so I had to resort to this idea so as not to be left with nothing like Luigi and Ciccantonio Vasquenz, since one must pay some debts. But they have to settle for a little at a time since they can't go to Aquila. I'm very sorry to have to disown a son, and I think about it a good deal and regret it a lot, but the fault is his and not mine, because I was forced to do it. Send me an envelope with his address and I'll write him a letter. Meanwhile, always try to avoid occasions for disagreement.
As to the case, perhaps it will not end at my timing, and perhaps not even at yours, if the magistrate doesn't kick the bucket. As it stands now it's impossible that the case will be decided. He should have done it yesterday, or rather January

27th and the session wasn't even held. All the cases for that day were postponed for April, but we don't yet know the exact day. "What goes slowly, goes well." Meanwhile, instead of celebrating Carnival we had to take the lawyer some pigeon eggs, and also 5 *lire*. Patience; here I am and I must see it out. It just bothers me that Francesco Perille won't wait any more; he absolutely wants something on account, or at least the interest. So far I've put him off by claiming that I had to wait for the case to be decided but now he's putting my back to the wall. I wrote you once before that you should write to him, but instead you didn't take any responsibility.

On January 6th I sent off an insured letter to you containing the copy of the mortgage inscription. I couldn't send you the copy of the document, not having been able to get it because I don't have enough money, but you don't need it for now, I can get it some other time.

Yesterday I sent a letter, or rather a plea, to His Majesty Victor Emmanuel III, begging him to grant the mercy of conditional freedom to Agostino. Let's hope he'll grant it to us, but I think it's very unlikely because we don't have any way to pull some strings. But I've tried my luck. I spent nothing for it, just a piece of paper for 1.25 and nothing else. If it works out, good; and if not, then face what we must.

I repeat, send me an envelope with Tommaso's address, because I'd like to write him a letter.

We are having spring-like weather. At the beginning of winter it looked as though we'd be buried in snow, but instead it was lovely weather all through December and January. We shall see what February brings...

First mention of Celestina, Angelo's wife-to-be. Her father had been a popular man in Cerchio, so everyone is delighted with the match. But the big news is that the case has finally been heard, a year and a half after it was initiated. Unfortunately, a technicality has delayed judgment, and we never do learn the result. The long-postponed creditor Perille has finally been paid.

My Dear Son,   April 2, 1913
With the greatest comfort I received your letter on the 19th of last month, in which I note your perfect state of health,

and also that of Celestina. Like you, we also enjoy it, but less so your mother who, as always, is indisposed with her familiar illness.

I would have replied sooner, but the money hadn't arrived yet, and so I waited until today. Fortunately, the money reached me on the 30th, just in time for me to go to the hearing at Celano. If it hadn't arrived I would have been staggering around without a nickel. On the 31st the case was finally heard and I had to pay the sum of £ 25.95 just for the stamped form and fee for the signature, in addition to 5 *lire* that I gave the lawyer on account, so in total I had to pay £30.95. Now we're waiting for publication of the sentence; we hope it will come out favorable, since the opposing lawyer based his defense on a falsehood, saying that the Torlonia Administration had made a deal with me and issued me a false copy of the contract, where the contract was registered in the books at Avezzano in 1910, and the sequestration was done in July 1911, and so the lawyer told me that the sentence might be delayed if they want to call someone from the Torlonia Administration as witness, but it will all be pointless.

As to the 128 *lire* you sent, I've already spent 69.45 of them without having bought myself even a loaf of bread – 30.95 for the case, and £ 38.50 to Signor Perille including interest, and the *reclamo*. I'm left with fifty-nine *lire* and thirty centimes, and those will go to pay the *fondiaria*, and half a *salma* of grain and maize that I got from Simplicio Tucceri more than a month ago, and to pay someone to plow the land in the Bacinetto, and once again we are left with nothing. Consequently, I beg you not to forget us, because other than what I've said above, that we're left with nothing, we have work to do in the Bacinetto. The grain has a lot of weeds and I have to work alone because your mother can't help, and I can barely drag myself along. Work, yes, but with difficulty; to do one day's work of a laborer I have to spend two. But I thank God that I can do this much, because I thought I could never work again, and so I repeat the plea I said above, so that after you have set up house don't forget to help and support your family, who are in the most extreme need, and also of advanced age. Today I count seventy years and five months. So the weight of our support is on your shoulders, and our hopes rest on you.

To redeem the house the Notary made me pay 71 *lire* just for the recording, and in addition to other things the tax collector gave me a surtax of another £ 37.82. I made several trips to Pescina; finally I managed to make the notary pay it because it was his mistake.

I won't go on. Let me know the day of your wedding, because we want to observe the day, and also have ourselves a little dinner party...

Angelo has gotten married, and Antonio rejoices with him, commenting on the wedding photograph and making a sly comment about a hoped-for pregnancy. Tommaso apparently got drunk and caused a scene at the wedding. Antonio also includes an affectionate note to the new daughter-in-law he knew as a child.

My Dear Son,   May 8, 1913

After a long silence I have finally received your long-awaited letter in which I see so much good news, and we are all very happy about it.

In the first place we congratulate you on your marriage and pray the Lord will keep you both always in perfect peace and calm, wishing you good fortune and happiness. Stay away from jealousy, and stay away from any occasion that might cause jealousy, and keep in mind that now you are a home-owner you have twice the responsibility, as it is my duty to give you this advice.

We are glad that the wedding feast went well, and glad of the honor given you by the participation of your fellow countrymen. As for Tommaso, as you said, he acted like a boor and I am also displeased, but at the same time I suggest you calm down, because you know what kind of person he is. Some disturbance was possible after the drinking and I even thought of mentioning it to you in my last letter, but decided not to after some thought.

You told me that your sister and niece should be at my dinner party and I did just that without your telling me, but because of business in the countryside we decided to have the dinner on the fifteenth, that is the feast of St. Isidoro.

We got the photographs and we still can't get enough of looking at them, and we are very glad to see you both looking so handsome, and with blooming health. We can't say that we are in perfect health, but we thank the Lord and pray him to keep us always as we are today, at least until your return, and then it's up to God. In your letter you said that Celestina was the same height as you, but in the photograph I saw that she is a little bit shorter. Your figures look the same to me, but since you are almost twice her age you will see that in a little while she will be the same height as you, and in figure she will come to surpass you.

Meanwhile let us pray to the Most Holy Virgin that everything will work out extremely well; have good judgment, and never forget the Most Holy Virgin. She has been and always will be your protectress, and we shall never cease to pray to her on your behalf...

On the back of the letter:

Our Dear Daughter Celestina,

We your father, mother, sister-in-law and niece have received the kisses you sent us in the card. Not being able for now to have the consolation of returning them to you face to face, we content ourselves with kissing your photograph, with the hope of being able to live on earth until your return, if the Lord grants it to me, and then we can get to know each other better when you aren't taken away from us again, to kiss each other and live together. We will love you as a daughter, the sister-in-law as a sister-in-law, and Marietta as an aunt, and you will love us as parents, sister-in-law and niece. Meanwhile receive many kisses and greetings from me, your mother, your sister-in-law and niece Marietta. Extend many greetings to your father and your mother, and your brother-in-law Vincenzo, and I anxiously hope on your return to kiss a baby boy in your arms. And so blessing you both, I am

Your Loving Father

Antonio Vasquenz

The case hasn't been decided yet because I didn't have a copy of the restraining order. It has to be done over. The date isn't set yet; a good result is hoped for.

Drought has destroyed the crops, with a fungal infection as the final touch. The decision on the case is still delayed. Cousin Vincenzo Pantano's wife is leaving to join him in America with her children (see Chapter 10 for more on the Pantano story) and the Vasquenz family takes advantage of this to have her carry a few little gifts to their sons. Antonio apologizes for asking for more money, but yet another need has arisen: the stable roof is about to cave in and must be repaired at once. Mariuccia has rebelled at last, refusing to live with her in-laws any more and writing an angry letter to her husband Vincenzo in America. This story and her letter are also covered in Chapter 10. Apparently she was so angry that she mutilated the letter.

My dear son,   June 21, 1913
    I hasten to reply to your letter that reached me on the 18th, giving you news of everything you want to know...We enjoy good health, but very upset about the bad harvest. After having sacrificed ourselves with efforts we have completely lost all the legumes from a terrible drought, so that they are cutting the fava to give the animals something to eat. Then our only hope rested on the grain but now we're also seeing a great failure to set seed, and it's impossible for them to fill out because they're dry from the base up to the last leaf, and the ear is the color of ashes. Yesterday evening there was a little rain, and this morning it finished the job with a thick fog and behold! in addition to drought there's rust.[98] I have based all my hopes on the beets, if the landlord will give something back to me.
    I got the £ 55 yesterday. They were all spent to pay the day-workers for winnowing the grain, and the *fondiaria* was due and I had thirty-six *soldi* left. I bought four kilos of bread and used it all up.
    As to the case, the magistrate couldn't hand down a definitive sentence because the copy of the distraint order didn't come in time. The case was reset for the twelfth of June, and was postponed to July seventh, and so I can't give you any result.
    We're glad that you've made peace with Tommaso again. Let me know some news about him. Since Vincenzo Pantano's

---

[98] *rugine.* The same word is used by American farmers to describe a fungus that gives a reddish stain to the infected plants.

wife is leaving on Monday we wanted to send you some bottles of liquor, but since she couldn't carry anything because she would be too burdened I'm sending you fifteen cigars, of which ten are for you, and five you are to give to your brother Tommaso in my name, if he will accept them, and greet him on my behalf. Agostino also greets him, and wants to know his address. He wrote me a few days ago and told me everything, and greets you. He hasn't answered you because he isn't allowed to write that often. In the package of cigars there is also another little packet containing 15 cigars, 10 from your sister and 5 from Lucia Pizitto. Give it to your brother-in-law Vincenzo. Pantano's wife is supposed to give Celestina a ring that your mother is sending her. She couldn't give her another present, so she begs her to accept this little gift. We hope to be among the living when you return, and then we can pay each other compliments.

And with this I come to beg you to reply to this letter immediately and send back something without fail. Despite the great family need I wouldn't have taken the liberty of asking anything from you, but a great necessity has compelled me to do it. In the first place in order to harvest a little grain because the hope for the fava has vanished. In the second place I have to spend about a hundred *lire* to fix the roof of the stable, if that will be enough, since I must replace four ropes that have broken, and then boards and gutters. As to the lime and sand, I can get them myself, but all the rest must be bought. The ropes alone will be 64 *lire* between door and timber. I tried the renter but he told me he couldn't pay me in advance because he's also very limited financially. And it's very necessary to do this, otherwise we'll have a cave-in and then it won't be possible to cover it again.

I'm sending you back the letter as you said. I have reproved your sister. She wouldn't tell me who rewrote it but from what she's told me she had good reason. He has never sent her a sympathetic letter, always complaints, and why? Because of the evil tongues of those in his family. She's eager to come to America to get away from those slanderous tongues. Beg her husband to send her the ticket, which we are also happy about and then you'll see that they'll do very well. You must know that your sister has gotten to the point you wouldn't recognize her. From the day of Ascension when she got this letter she hasn't been in good health. She was in bed six days with a fever and now she's convalescent she can't earn a nickel. She will write you separately and tell you everything....I couldn't make anything of the scratched out letters and even she doesn't know.

Two and a half years intervene before the last letter in the collection. Antonio must have written dozens over this time but they were not kept with this collection and have been lost. This letter makes no mention of what must have been the biggest news during the gap: on January 15, 1915 a massive earthquake destroyed 80% of the structures in Cerchio, killing 10% of the population. Beyond that, the last letter is not a happy ending for the family either: Angelo no longer shows interest in his family and hasn't written for months, one of his brothers has died, and Mariuccia's husband Vincenzo is at the front, leaving her with nothing to live on.

My dear ungrateful son, the stranger,   February 26, 1916
    I would never have believed that you could forget your father, your mother, your sister and your brother. I'm not saying that you should send us money all the time, I don't ask that of you any more, but do you remember anything of what I taught you? I sent you to school with my old friend Luca, and to Giovanni Vitale to teach you how to write. I have sent you two letters since Ciccantonio [Francesco Antonio Vasquenz, probably a cousin of Antonio] returned and haven't deserved any response. Recall that you haven't written since May, and yet I will risk writing you a third and if I don't get a reply this will be the last. I said that you have forgotten your brother because after the letter in which I told you about his death you didn't have the courtesy to reply even to comfort me and your mother. I said you have forgotten your sister because her husband has gone as a soldier and she has nothing to live on. You should repay the money to her husband. You could have sent 10 *lire* at a time and that would make her happy. I say no more; if you have the courage you will do as I say.
I greet you and wish you a thousand blessings from Heaven and I am
                    Your Loving Father,
                    Antonio

Chapter 10
THE PRICE OF EMIGRATION

In addition to Antonio's letters, the Vasquenz collection at Western Reserve Historical Society contains a dozen miscellaneous letters from other relatives. Among these are several which paint a vivid picture of the difficulties borne by women whose men have been far away for years.

When Angelo came back in late 1909 he began a clandestine love affair with his cousin Marietta Vasquenz. It seems to have been a very chaste affair, but Marietta was desperately in love with him and devastated when he went back to America. Two drafts of a letter from Angelo to Marietta indicate that he cared for her also, and made some attempt to keep the relationship alive. But he didn't write often enough to soothe her anxiety, which dominates her letters as she begins to realize that he is not coming back. Her family, wiser than she, tried to discourage the attachment, but she clung to her hopes. When Angelo did write, his words failed to reassure her – perhaps intentionally, if he was trying to disabuse her – and in her last letter (July 1910, only five months after he left) she pours out her hurt and anger.

Marietta's letters are long, rambling, and intensely personal. She was literate and therefore had no need to restrain her language as she might have done with a scribe. After one hundred years, it still seems an invasion of privacy to repeat them, but in the interests of sympathetic scholarship some extracts may be given.

My beloved cousin,   April 6, 1910
    How great was my joy, O my beloved...how happy I was to get your letter, I can't find words to describe it to you. I kissed and rekissed a thousand times the writing that brought me such glad tidings of your successful trip. Now my torments will

115

end; once again I have seen the adored page written by your hands... But know, my dear, that our love has been discovered by my sisters who are warning me, saying that you are deceiving me when you write, and that you won't come back any more. Tell me if you love me, Angelo, I don't believe that you are deceiving me, if you love me as much as I love you, write it to me, repeat it a thousand times and then from your writing I can grant myself the calm that I can't enjoy as long as you are far from me...

My Angelo,   May(?) 3, 1910

Finding myself at the moment with no occupation I will occupy myself with you, since I don't even know myself now that I can't see you. Deprived of your presence I try to fool myself by writing these few and badly-formed lines, with the same pleasure that I would have if I were speaking to you. My dear, I'm not writing this for no reason, I just want to know why you are so slow in writing. I have no doubts, because I know that you are true to me; but who knows, perhaps you have changed, perhaps you have forgotten my love. Ah! Angelo, do you remember how I loved you? Do you remember when I asked you, "Angelo, when will you write to me?" and you said, "Every day" and now why do you delay so much? Do you remember when I loved you so much that I couldn't do anything without seeing you? And now with what heart, with what nerve do you leave me? I think I will love you always, always...My weeping eyes are in constant vigil, waiting for the moment that I receive your letter with the picture in it. My afflicted heart desires nothing but you. The sighs that escape me every time I think of you while I'm working – and that is every moment – my imagination that pictures to me no other object but my Angiolino, the laments I make to Heaven of the intense torments that give me no peace until I see you – they are at least proofs of what I write to you...Reassure me that you love me always. I will guard your letter like a jewel, I will read it a thousand thousand times a day and suffer my pains with less impatience...My dear, I must tell you that here I am suffering worse than before you left. They've done so much to discourage my feelings for you and nothing has succeeded, and so they won't do anything more for me, they won't give me clothing or shoes, telling me to do it for myself. They wouldn't even give me money for the stamp to mail this to you...They keep saying that you won't write to me and that they're glad...

She included a photograph of herself with this letter, asking for one from him in return. Apparently he never sent it.

My beloved Angelo,   June 29, 1910
In the constant false hope of receiving your news, as I diligently send you mine, I have been waiting for several days with the most lively impatience. Can it be possible that other interests, other thoughts occupy your mind, after all the protestations you made me? Your behavior, now so uncertain and irregular, is not like that of before, when you said you were in love with me and claimed that you couldn't think of anyone else but me. Now I realize too late that it was all lies to lure me into loving you; once you saw that I was attached to you and in love you thought no more of me. You have changed if you need to deceive me. If I have become a nuisance for you, why not cut off cleanly a love that has become unpleasant to you?...I can't stay still a minute, I tell you, without thinking of you, my only love. I just ask myself, speaking to you, "Why don't you write? Why don't you send me your news?" You can't imagine, my dear, how your Marietta suffers and languishes when she doesn't hear from you.

My Treasure,   July 1, 1910
If I could blaze a clear trail to the bottom of your heart and penetrate its most inaccessible secrets, then I could see for myself what you truly are and my fears would vanish in a moment. This quest being completely impossible for me, I must trust in your assertions which I hope are perfectly truthful and honest. But I fall into the thought that your feelings in regard to me are a little bit different than those you showed in your last letter. So don't fail to show them to me with one of your dear and prompt replies, which I am awaiting as soon as possible...In your reply explain yourself fully, speak to me as if you were before me, reveal all your feelings, for in short only you and I will read it, and certainly no one will know our secrets, and we can make ourselves two bodies with one soul. Write

me long letters until your heart can't think of anything more to say, and I will do the same...

This letter is undated, but from the tone it is probably the last of those preserved. It is difficult to follow her agitated writing, but it seems that Angelo had sent a letter which she interpreted (correctly or not) as a rejection.

Angelo Dearest,

Now I'm going to tell you that in your letter I see that you don't love me any more as you did and now you don't love me any more. Then you tell me I had the nerve to write you two letters and a postcard. Bravo! So that's what I deserve! After having loved you with the most lively sincerity I deserve thanks. If I knew that my portrait was not received with passion I would not have sent it to you, and I sent you the card to wish you a happy name-day,[99] and that's very proper... Then what really made me furious was learning that whenever you wrote you were just teasing me. How could I say this after getting your letters? Certainly I would not have said it. I said it now because I see that you are careless. I feel sorry for you that you are made as you say you are: the idea you can't see me and you positively don't write me. Another thing that makes me laugh: that you can't get a photograph because of the heat. Now I see that you think I'm stupid...You should think of just one thing: that in 5 months I've had 3 wretched letters – what are you doing?...Moreover, you should have realized that I am not just anybody, I am your cousin and you shouldn't have deceived me in this way...

A story with a happier ending is that of the Pantano family. Vincenzo Pantano was a cousin of Angelo, and first emigrated in February 1906, going to Ernest, PA. He returned to Cerchio for an unknown period, and then left again in late December 1909, going to Mount Carmel, PA to join his cousin Tommaso. By April 1910 he was in Republic, PA with Angelo and the others, probably also

---

[99] The *onomastico* (day of the saint who has the same name as the individual) is often celebrated with more attention than the date of birth.

working in the coal mines. Vincenzo was illiterate and apparently did not write home very often. A letter to Vincenzo from his wife Domenica has been preserved in the Vasquenz collection. Evidence in the letters suggests that the Cerchio men may all have shared a single mail box, and if Angelo was the only literate one he may have been asked to read letters for the others.

Domenica is more decorous than Marietta – she seems to have been the proper submissive wife and she blames herself for her anxiety, which still manages to break through. By this point Vincenzo had been away a year and a half.

> Dearest Spouse,   August 18, 1911
>   I write you a couple of lines to let you know that we are well, as I hope is true for you. Dear husband, I would like to know why you put off writing to me so long, keeping me always worrying. I beg you to let me know your news every 15 days, since you know what I'm like. The boy has been sick since August 2nd, yet you leave me hanging by not letting me know your news and so I must be always troubled and you know very well what our sons are like when they don't feel well. They make me do penance not only by day but also by night. But it's enough for me if you are well. I don't beat the boys because if you have sons you will always be troubled because no sooner does one get well than the other gets sick. But I repeat, if God gives you health it's enough and I'm happy.
>   I don't have anything more to tell you. Take care of your health and make me a little more happy by letting me know your news often.
>   Greetings from your mother to you and to Giovanni, greetings from our sons, and greetings from your loving wife
> Domenica Pantano

Vincenzo remained uncommunicative, although he probably did write occasionally. But by the end of 1912 his mother, Angelo's aunt Maria Giuseppa Cipriani, was so concerned that she wrote a letter directly to her nephew, dictated to Antonio, in which she asks for news of her son. She fears that something terrible may have happened to him, a fear that must have been constantly present when a letter did not arrive after weeks of waiting.

Dear Angiolino,   Dec. 13, 1912

For a long time I haven't received any news at all from my son Vincenzo Pantano. I waited until today with much impatience, and still nothing. Consequently I implore you to let me know something about him, because I don't pass a moment that I'm not worrying about this delay in writing, so you must have the kindness to keep me informed about everything, be it good or bad, and I will be very obliged to you. His wife is always weeping, as am I – imagine how we feel. I repeat, don't fail to do me this favor. The thought we have is that in Cerchio they're saying he is in prison. I don't believe it, and his wife knows nothing of this as yet, but the delay of this time makes me doubt that what they say may be true. Not only do we weep, but his children weep in seeing their mother weep. I implore you to reply at once so that we can free ourselves from so much sadness...

I send you my greetings and renewing the prayer above I am –

Your Affectionate, Maria Giuseppa Cipriani

P.S. from Antonio: If some accident has happened to Vincenzo Pantano, and money is needed don't fail to let us know everything and try to help him so that everything is made good.

By spring of 1913 Vincenzo had managed to save enough to send Domenica the fare so that she and the two boys could come to America. They left Cerchio in June 1913, bearing small gifts and probably letters from the Cerchiese, as we learn from Antonio's letter of June 21, 1913. The 1920 census shows them living in Redstone, PA with three more children. Vincenzo was still working as a coal miner.[100]

---

[100] Vincenzo and Domenica Pantano and five children; Sheet 4B, lines 70-76, Enumeration District 76, Redstone Township, Fayette County, Pennsylvania; Pennsylvaian Census of Population; *Fourteenth Census of the United States, 1920* (National Archives Microfilm Publication T625, roll 1570); Records of the Bureau of the Census, Record Group 29. Accessed through Ancestry.com.

The last case is that of Angelo's sister Mariuccia, who was having a rough time of it in Cerchio since her husband, Vincenzo di Domenico, left. We do not know how long he was away — ship manifests show several men with this name arriving from Cerchio — but he was already in Republic when Antonio's letters begin. Mariuccia was helping her elderly parents and caring for her sickly daughter Antonetta while living with her in-laws. The cliché is that women never get along with their daughters-in-law, and it certainly was the case here. It seems that Signora di Domenico was not slow to write her son about his wife's perceived failings, and Vincenzo believed his mother and wrote harsh letters to Mariuccia, reproving her for her failings. Mariuccia's spirit boiled at the injustice, as we see in several of Antonio's letters. Finally, in spring 1913 after a particularly bad interval, he suggested that she write to her brother, in hopes that he could mediate between husband and wife. Mariuccia, who was illiterate, dictated a letter with no holds barred, in which she makes a plea that must have been that of many abandoned wives: to be brought to America to build a new life with her husband.

Dear brother,   June 19, 1913
    ...I've been sharply reproved by our father because of the letter I'm sending back enclosed, and why I burned it. Dear brother, you would have done worse if it had been you, wrongly slandered and your honor so greatly accused, and being humiliated by your husband. The burned letter means that if his family don't stop criticizing me, especially his mother, I'll have to take drastic steps because not only do they talk about me in Cerchio, they also write to him and he believes them and keeps sending me upsetting letters. One time he treated me as a shameful woman and why? Because I was acting badly. In another he wrote me that she had acted as a good woman, because he was ashamed to hear more bad news about me, and that the whole town was amazed by my bad behavior. Another time because I had an *arca* made to hold a bit of bread when I have any. He sent me a letter that made me weep night and day, treating me like a fashionista. He took away the house in the piazza he had bought me, and also a *machinetta* [some

small kitchen appliance]. Another time he wrote that he wasn't working in America to get food for me and everybody else, because they told him that I gave my father some food. Let him say how much money he sent me that I could spend as I wished. There are so many other things that I can't remember them all, but this last one in which he tells me not to go out at night, that I should stay home after sunset – who does he take me for? Maybe the daughters of Master Pietro? Two years ago when our mother was ill, everything that we needed had to go to pay off Francesco Perille. Could our father go around getting what she needed? Of course not; and because I went, his mother had the nerve to say that I went to get myself a glass of wine every morning, and to make it clearer to you, she said that she saw me with it. I can be kindhearted to her but you can be sure that if it's not one thing, it'll be another and then I'll go to join Agostino [she will do something drastic that will land her in prison]. And he believes everything she writes. Why doesn't he find out from some goodhearted people in town before giving me such distress? For instance, Aunt Lucia, who knows about her and will know everything about my conduct. She remembers that one time she was there when she told me that she couldn't go out in Cerchio and if she did she had to cover her face because of my bad behavior. He was there then, we were all together as a family, such was my bad behavior, so if you consider that she said it to me when he was there you can imagine what she can say now that he is far away and she's trying to make trouble between us. There are two of them in Cerchio who want to do this, one is she and the other is our Signora Aunt Grazia Serchia. Every time they go to mass they plot how to make trouble between husband and wife, and for fifteen weeks after they've had communion on Saturday they go to wash out their mouths with a little drink. They're trying to tar me with their brush, but they won't succeed because it won't stick.

This letter could go on but since I'm embarrassed to bore the scribe any more I'll just tell you one last thing and you can be the judge. If you had a wife in Cerchio, and we had sowed a field with grain, and our father cultivated it by hand and you sent the money for the sowing, winnowing and reaping, and then when it was time to thresh you were to write our father and say "Thresh the grain and keep it all for yourself", could your wife ever look you in the face? Would you have the heart to do it? Or to put it another way, would it be a good thing that your father should eat fine white bread while your wife labors to buy herself a kilo of cornmeal? I think not, so you be the judge, think about it and pass your sentence. That's what my husband did; he wrote to his father "Don't sell the grapes; keep them for yourself to drink wine". There you have the passion of a husband for his wife, so the only way to make things better between us is for him to get me out of his family's sight. Here in Cerchio we don't have any worldly goods, we don't have houses or fields, the harvest is very bad, things cost a good deal. So let him bring me to America, we'll stay five or six years, make some money and then decide depending on the situation we're in. Otherwise if we stay in Cerchio we'll have to pay a high price for the rent and things to live on, and go as day-laborers to earn a pittance. So talk to him about it so he can send me a ticket, and I'm sure we'll always have a happy life. In any case I tell you I absolutely won't go back to his family.

But Vincenzo ignored her plea, and himself came back to Italy, possibly after the outbreak of World War I when many émigrés returned to fight for their country. We don't know what happened after that; the last we hear of them is Antonio's letter of February 1916, in which he says that Vincenzo is away as a soldier and Mariuccia has nothing to live on.

In fact, we do not know the end of the story for any of the Vasquenz family. The lives of "important" people are more or less well documented from birth to death; the vast majority of the human race live and die in obscurity, unknown to history. Or they may appear once, briefly, as minor actors in some event, and then sink from sight. Anglo-Saxons describe the soul as a bird that comes from the night into a brightly lighted hall, and then flies out again — from darkness into darkness. Through a fortunate sequence of events these letters have been preserved, opening a window onto four years in the life of one family who persevered through large disasters and small joys, living their lives as best they could. We can be sure that while discouragement often overcame him, Antonio Vasquenz did not go gentle into that long good night. He fought for his family as long as he lived, and thanks to his letters his memory can be preserved far longer than he ever imagined.

Appendix I
SAMPLE OF ANTONIO'S LETTERS

The following is a direct transcription of Antonio's letter of March 17, 1911, describing the death of his daughter Pasquala. Accent marks, capitals and other punctuation are also those used by him.

Cerchio, 17 Marzo 1911 — Caro figlio —
Con sommo mio rammarico, e di tutta la nostra famiglia ti dò con la presente l'infausta notizia della morte della tua Sorella Pasquccia avvenuta il giorno dieci corrente, alla mezza dopo mezzo giorno, confortata da tutti i divini sacramenti pacificamente rese la Benedetta anima sua nella braccia del Signore lasciando ci afflitti, e sconsolati per la perduta di una da noi tanta amata, ma non è così però dalla Suocera, e dal suo Marito che qui appresso ti farò consapevole del tutto. Tu intando consolati come ci abbiamo consolati noi, in primo perchè fece una morte cosi bella, posso dire che mori informa di Angelo, nel raccomandarci l'anima essa si faceva la croce ogni volta che il Sacerdote dava la Benedizione, infine domandò se quando altro tempo ci era a morire, ed escalmò Lo quanto è lunga! ed all'istante spirò senza farcene nemmeno accorgere

Il secondo motivo posso assicurarti che l'anno fatto morire di debolezza, ed anche di crepacuore, e per questo noi ci abbiamo consolati; e cosi persuaditi anche tu, e consolatene perche a finito di patire e di tribulare nelle mani di quella gente ingrate, senza cuore e senza passione. Passo ora a raccontarti tutte le ingratitudine che il marito, e la Suocera ci anno fatto, non solo in vita, ma anche dopo morta. Non appena ritornato il Marito per pochi giorni seguitò a custodirla come prima, quando a veduto che la malatia era inguaribile non l'à più curata, non ci à pigliato più un soldo di latte, non più un soldo di vino, non più una mezza libra di Carne, è stata costretta di rimangiare i cibi correnti che mangiavano essi, schifata dal Marito, e dalla Suocera, la cucchiara, la forchetta, il piatto, e la bocoletta con l'acqua da parte senza che essa avesse potuto andare a pigliarsi l'acqua nella conca e bevere col maniere, segnalate tutte le cose per timore che non si avesse pigliato qualchè mezzo chilo di mazzocche e cambiarsele con qualchè mela, o pera, lasciata più molti, e molti giorni sola senza lasciarci qualchè cosa da manciare, qualchè giorno che la sapeva tua Madre, ci andava, e ci portava qualchè cosa, e quanto non sapeva niente passava le giornate senza manciare, e tante, e tante aldre cose che io la tralascio, e questo perchè lo faceva? lo faceva acciochè essa mi avesse forzato a me, e gli avesse ridato le duecento lire, e gli avesse finito di darci la dote, se tuttoquesto io lo avesse saputo prima, cosi malata come si trovava me la sarei riportata con me, essa diceva a tutti che gli volevano bene, e che non ci facevano mancare niente, ma questo però lo diceva per non essere abbandonata totalmente, basta dirti che la matina dei dieci si confessò, e dopo portataci la comunione lasciò la felice memoria quasi agonizante e se ne andò a vancare senza trovarsi presente quanto spirò, più volte mi domandò se era ritornato Giovanni ma chi te lo dà? dopo ritornato la trovò morta non fù uomo di andarci in faccia, e nemmeno di buttare una lacrima, ne esso, e nemeno la sua Madre, ma pensò solo a dare ordine alla figlia di Bazziere di farci levare gli orecchini nelle orecchie nascostamente da noi, e siccome la felice memoria si aveva più volte raccomandata a Mariuccia dicendoci che non l'avesse abbandonata e che non ci avesse fatto levare niente ma che l'avesse vestita come aveva uscita da casa, pure con tutto questo la figlia di Bazziere nel mentre la stavano a mettere nella cassa ebbe la temerità strappargle gli orecchini dall orecchie la matina io scoppai la cassa e vedeto che non ci erano gli obligai a farceli rimettere, non basta questo ci è ancora da dire più sensibile, siccome che in quel giorno si incontrò la casualità che il Prete doveva fare due funerali, uno per la felice memoria, e l'aldro per Giuseppe Antidormi osia Pompei, essendo un solo prete non poteva fare due funzioni, mi disse cosi, oggi si funziona per il morto, e lundi per la morta, o pure se sei contendo applicherò la messa di oggi per tutti due, e la messa di lunedi anche per tutti due, io gli risposi di si, e feci sapere per mezzo di Brizio che la riuscita non poteva farsi lunedi perchè ci era il funerale da farsi, la risposta di Brizio fù che la riuscita si faceva il settimo giorno, la Domenica ad un'ora tardi seppe per casualità che si faceva la riuscita, e siccome ne noi e nemmeno nesuno dei nostri Parenti, per assicurarmi mandai Mariuccia la tua Cugina a domandarlo ad esso sai cosa ci rispose (io fò la riuscita domani, se loro non si trovano comodi se la facciano per conto loro, ed a comodo loro,) esso, e la stega sua Madre aveva avvisato solo uno, o due parenti suoi, senza avvisare nesuno dei nostri sempre per causa dei orecchini, e poi voleva che noi di casa, ed i nostri parenti possimo andati nella sua casa a pigliarlo e portarlo in chiesa, tutto questo non era convenienza la nostra, io non feci aldro chiamai all'improvviso pochi parenti, e tutti i nostri vicini andamono alla messa e riuscito dalla Chiesa ritornamono tutti a casa, esso si è insuperbilo per questo, e a detto che non voleva essere più chiamato da noi e che veggo che cosa posso fare per la 200 £: Non posso più scrivere, e ti prego leggere più volte la presente perchè ci sono dei errori, e mancano dei punti, e delle virgole perciò bisogna rifletterla più volte, ci sarebbero tante aldre cose da dire sù questo ma nel mentre stavo scrivento mi anno sfuggito di mente. Solo ti dico di non trattarlo più ne per amico, e nemmeno per cognato, ma bensi ritenerlo per il primo inemico capitale del mondo.

Voglio dirti un proverbio che dicevano gli antichi ed è questo: L'uomo con i peli rossi non lo portare in casa se non lo conosci. Ed un'aldro è questo. Per conoscere bene una persona ti ci devi manciare un tomolo di sale insieme.

Possiamo quasi dire che tu ci ai bazzicato un bel poco di tempo insieme, e forse lo avrai consumato una buona quantità di sale con esso e non ancora lo ai scoverto che persona è quello, se io lo avessi conosciuto prima non ci avrei data la felice memoria nemmeno se avesse tenuto un milione alla Posta, del resto è fatto, e non può più ripararcesi, Pasquccia possa stare alla Gloria del Paradiso ed essi possano pagare tuttociò che ci anno fatto di male.

Passo a darti i miei più cari saluti, come pure quei di tua Madre, ed i tua Sorella Mariuccia, da parte di noi saluterai ancora Vincenzo, ed in particolare lo saluta sua Moglie Mariuccia, fammi sapere qualchè cosa di tuo fratello Tommaso, ripetendoti i miei, con al S: benedizione mi dico

Il Tuo Aff— Padre
Antonio Vasquenz

Appendix II
COST OF LIVING AND CURRENCY CONVERSION

Within a nation the price of an item changes over time as a result of the changing buying power of the currency with respect to some standard (inflation and deflation). In the 1950's a candy bar cost 5¢, today the same piece of candy costs 89¢. The relative price of different goods also changes over time as a function of government actions (price controls, taxes) and the balance between supply and demand. During a prolonged period of drought the cost of bread will be higher than during a time of plenty. An item produced in limited numbers by a new technology when costs of production are high will be more expensive (in constant dollars) than the equivalent item some years later when production has been made more efficient and a much larger number are available. Personal computers are a good example of the latter case. Price comparisons between two nations in the same time period depend not only on the relative buying power of the currency in each country but also, again, on production costs and supply/demand in each country. When the dollar is strong relative to the yen, a camera purchased in Japan is a good buy; when the dollar is weak the same camera becomes relatively more expensive for the American. On the other hand, beef is always more available in America than it is in Japan, so that beef is always relatively inexpensive in the United States compared with Japan, regardless of exchange rates.

Given these considerations, it might seem pointless to convert Antonio's costs in 1910 *lire* into modern dollars. However, it does provide a way to grasp the *relative* cost of items to Antonio in units familiar to the reader. The table below shows a series of Antonio's costs and the equivalent value in modern U.S. dollars (for methods, see discussion below). The cost of a single item here is less useful than the relationship between two expenses. For instance, a single bottle of coffee costs more than a day's wage for a woman pulling weeds in the fields, and that woman earns 1/3 to 1/6 as much as field workers during the reaping season. The female day-laborer would have to work for four to five days to pay a notary to copy a document for her, while filing the original document would represent up to 75 days of labor. A donkey, or even a mare, costs Antonio less than having the wheels of his cart repaired, while a sheet of letter paper costs four times as much as a flask of unfermented wine – a result of the high taxes on paper and the fact that the wine was purchased from a fellow villager and may have been "under the table" and not subject to taxes.

Item Cited by Antonio	Cost to Antonio (1910 *lire*)	Equivalent (2006 *lire*)	Equivalent (2006 US$)
1 egg	1.5 soldi	515	0.35
Flask of wine, unfermented	6 soldi	2,070	1.40
Sheet of letter paper	1.25 lire	8,610	5.85
Daily wages, field worker	30 soldi	10,335	7.00
4 kilos of bread	36 soldi	12,400	8.45
Bottled coffee	2.25 lire	15,500	10.55
Daily wages, reapers	5-9.5 lire	34,450-65,450	23.50-44.60
Copy of a document	6-7 lire	41,340-48,230	28.20-32.85
Plowing services	20-27 lire	137,800-186,020	93.90-126.75
Comune tax	30 lire	206,690	140.85
One *salma* of seed	35 lire	241,135	164.30
Donkey	60 lire	413,376	281.70
Mare	70 lire	482,270	328.65
Recording mortgage	71 lire	489,160	333.35
Repair cart wheels	75 lire	516,720	352.15
Filing *reclamo*	100 lire	688,960	469.50
Filing mortgage documents	113 lire	778,525	530.55
Annual lease on fields	310 lire	2,135,775	1455.50
Purchase of house	2000 lire	13,779,200	9390.20

(Amounts for 2006 have been rounded to simplify reading)

METHODS

ISTAT, the Italian Bureau of National Statistics, has developed coefficients based on the consumer's price index to compare the buying power of the *lira* between any two years from 1860 (unification) to 2006 (the last year that the *lira* was accepted as legal tender). The buying power of the *lira* did not change appreciably between 1910 and 1913; the 1910 value is used throughout the table above. A useful on-line conversion can be found at:

http://www.cracantu.it/servizi/on_line/vari/valorelira.php

provided by the Cassa Rurale ed Artigiana di Cantù, a credit union established in 1907. The buying power of one *lira* in 1910 corresponded to 6,889.6 *lire* in 2006.

There are many web sites listing daily rates for currency conversions in recent years. Values shown above were calculated for December 31, 2006 at: http://www.xe.com/ict/

Conversion of 1903 pounds sterling to modern U.S. dollars (cited in Chapter 6) used calculations provided by the Economic History Association at: http://eh.net/hmit with the option "Computing 'Real Value' Over Time With a Conversion Between U. K. Pounds and U. S. Dollars, 1830-2007".

Appendix III
PROVERBS AND SAYINGS

Like many *contadini*, Antonio is fond of proverbs. Sometimes he signalizes them with quotation marks and attributes them to a friend or to "the ancients". In other cases there is no such indication, but his words have the quality of being a well-known saying. The original Italian is given to provide a sense of Antonio's dialectical spelling and grammar.

"*visitare gli infermi - visitare i Carcerati - e seppellire i morti*" Spring 1910
    "Visit the sick, visit the imprisoned, and bury the dead" (*Misericordia Corporale*)

"*mentre ci è lo spirito ci è la speranza*" Sept. 25, 1910
    "While there's life there's hope" (Proverb)

"*dove si casca, casca, e dove si more, more*" Sept. 25, 1910
    "Where you fall, you fall and where you die, you die" (Nicola Ciaglia)

"*4 pagnotte, ed una buona fiasca pigliamoci il mondo come casca*" Nov. 25, 1910
    "Four loaves and a good flask and we'll take the world as it comes." (Nicola Ciaglia)

"*L'uomo con i peli rossi non lo portare in casa se non lo conosci*" Mar. 17, 1911
    "Never bring a man with red hair into the house if you don't know him". (the ancients)

"Per conoscere bene una persona ti ci devi manciare un tomolo di sale insieme" Mar. 17, 1911

"To know a person well you must eat a *tomolo* of salt with him" (the ancients)

"quando si guadagna qualchè tozzo di pane se lo mancia, e quando non a niente digiuna" May 10, 1911

"When he earns a bit of bread he eats it and when he has nothing he fasts" (said of Isodoro Ninuccio)

"quello che l'anno mena, l'anno locora" Aug. 15, 1912

"What the year brings, the year consumes"

"venca tardi, e venca bene" Jan. 29, 1913

"What goes slowly, goes well."

"se guarisce quella risuscitano i morti" Aug. 15, 1910

"if she gets well, the dead can rise"

"non ci è modo da poter riparare ai piccoli picci per la cattiva raccolda". Sept. 25, 1910

"there's no way to make up for a bad harvest with little bits"

"quando me chiama bisogna che vado, e non ci è rimedio" June 27, 1911.

"when He calls me I must go, and there's nothing to be done about it"

"ora che mi ci trovo bisogna che ballo — ma se mi tocca balleranno loro" Aug.17, 1911

"Now I have to dance to their tune, but if it's up to me they'll be the ones to dance"

"*ma se dovesse risarchire il danno non ci basterebbe il Paradiso se avesse chi veselo comprasse*" Sept. 27, 1912

"if one must pay the damages Paradise would not be enough even if there were someone who wanted to buy it"

REFERENCES

BOOKS

Felice, Costantino, *Verde a Mezzogiorno: L'agricoltura abruzzese dall'Unità a oggi* [Green to the South: Abruzzo Agriculture from Unification to Today]. Donzelli Editore, Rome, 664 pp., 2007.

King, Bolton and Thomas Okey, *Italy Today*, Charles Scribner's Sons, New York, 1913. Description by English authors of Italian political and social issues with good chapters on poverty, agriculture and peasant life, education, industry, the role of the church etc.

Villari, Luigi, *Italian Life in Town and Country*, G.P. Putnam and Sons, New York, 1903. Overview of life in Italy, chapters cover social classes, wealth and poverty, political and religious life, agriculture, artisans, legal structures, festivals and amusements, etc.

ARTICLES

Linoli, Antonio (English translation by Ken Hurry), The Fucino: Draining of a major lake in the second half of the XIXth century. Proceedings of ICID 21st European Regional Conference, 2005, pp. 167-186, published on-line at:
www.zalf.de/icid/ICID_ERC2005/HTML/ERC2005PDF/History_Session/Linoli_3.pdf

Piccardi, Luigi, Yves Gaudemer, Paul Tapponnier and Mario Boccaletti, Active oblique extension in the central Apennines (Italy): evidence from the Fucino region. Geophys. J. Int. 139, 499-530 (1999). Available on-line at: adsabs.harvard.edu/full/1999 GeoJI.139.499P

www.abruzzomio.it - Italian-language site about the Abruzzo. Includes history, tourist guide, food, arts and festivals, folklore, proverbs.

www.cerchio.terremarsicane.it - Italian-language site for village of Cerchio. Includes sections on the history of the village, customs and costumes, festivals

cerchio.it.gg - Jazzy Italian-language site about Cerchio, founded by homesick native son. Sections maintained by different people include a dialect vocabulary list, list of surnames, photos, proverbs.

Figure 1. Base map of Italy showing outlines of regions. Box in center shows location of Figure 2.[101]

Figure 2. Topographic map of the area, showing towns and principal features.

Figure 3. Family tree showing individuals mentioned in the letters. Solid lines show relationships supported by documentary evidence; dashed line for Pietro is a reasonable inference (see discussion in text).

---

[101] Base map kindly provided from
http://english.freemap.jp/europe_e/italy_kouiki_1.html. Accessed February 22, 2012.

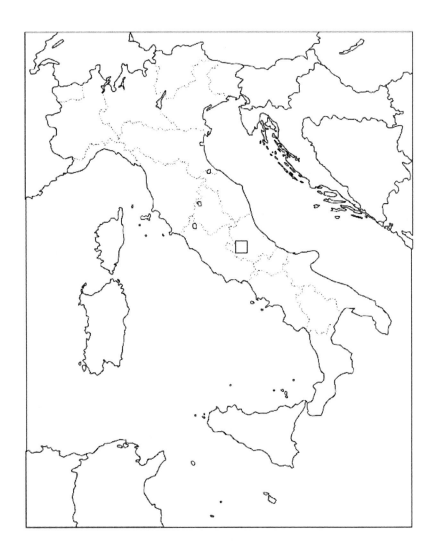

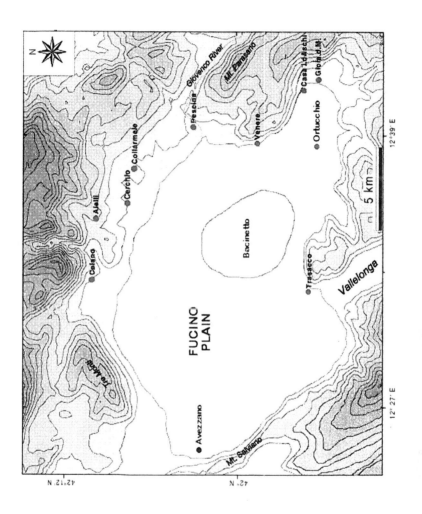

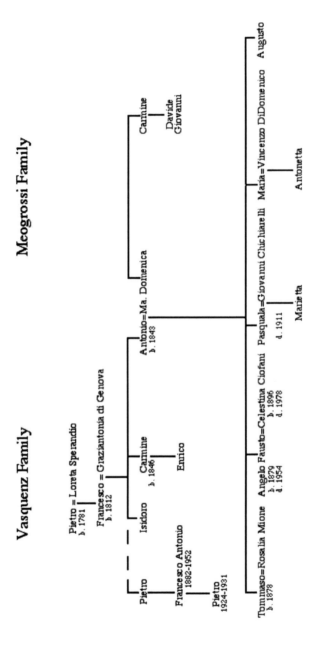

Vasquenz Family

Meogrossi Family

VIA FOLIOS

A refereed book series dedicated to the culture of Italians and Italian Americans.

MICHAEL PARENTI. *Waiting for Yesterday: Pages from a Street Kid's Life.* Vol 90 Memoir. $15

ANNIE LANZILOTTO, *Schistsong*, Vol. 89. Poetry, $15

EMANUEL DI PASQUALE, *Love Lines*, Vol. 88. Poetry, $10

CAROSONE & LOGIUDICE. *Our Naked Lives.* Vol 87 Essays. $15

JAMES PERICONI. *Strangers in a Strange Land: A Survey of Italian-Language American Books.* Vol. 86. Book History. $24

DANIELA GIOSEFFI, *Escaping La Vita Della Cucina*, Vol. 85. Essays & Creative Writing. $22

MARIA FAMÀ, *Mystics in the Family*, Vol. 84. Poetry, $10

ROSSANA DEL ZIO, *From Bread and Tomatoes to Zuppa di Pesce "Ciambotto"*, Vol. 83. $15

LORENZO DELBOCA, *Polentoni*, Vol. 82. Italian Studies, $15

SAMUEL GHELLI, *A Reference Grammar*, Vol. 81. Italian Language. $36

ROSS TALARICO, *Sled Run*, Vol. 80. Fiction. $15

FRED MISURELLA, *Only Sons*, Vol. 79. Fiction. $14

FRANK LENTRICCHIA, *The Portable Lentricchia*, Vol. 78. Fiction. $16

RICHARD VETERE, *The Other Colors in a Snow Storm*, Vol. 77. Poetry. $10

GARIBALDI LAPOLLA, *Fire in the Flesh*, Vol. 76 Fiction & Criticism. $25

GEORGE GUIDA, *The Pope Stories*, Vol. 75 Prose. $15

ROBERT VISCUSI, *Ellis Island*, Vol. 74. Poetry. $28

ELENA GIANINI BELOTTI, *The Bitter Taste of Strangers Bread*, Vol. 73, Fiction, $24

PINO APRILE, *Terroni*, Vol. 72, Italian Studies, $20

EMANUEL DI PASQUALE, *Harvest*, Vol. 71, Poetry, $10

ROBERT ZWEIG, *Return to Naples*, Vol. 70, Memoir, $16

AIROS & CAPPELLI, *Guido*, Vol. 69, Italian/American Studies, $12

FRED GARDAPHÉ, *Moustache Pete is Dead! Long Live Moustache Pete!*, Vol. 67, Literature/Oral History, $12

PAOLO RUFFILLI, *Dark Room/Camera oscura*, Vol. 66, Poetry, $11

HELEN BAROLINI, *Crossing the Alps*, Vol. 65, Fiction, $14

COSMO FERRARA, *Profiles of Italian Americans*, Vol. 64, Italian Americana, $16

GIL FAGIANI, *Chianti in Connecticut*, Vol. 63, Poetry, $10

BASSETTI & D'ACQUINO, *Italic Lessons*, Vol. 62, Italian/American Studies, $10

CAVALIERI & PASCARELLI, Eds., *The Poet's Cookbook*, Vol. 61, Poetry/Recipes, $12

EMANUEL DI PASQUALE, *Siciliana*, Vol. 60, Poetry, $8

NATALIA COSTA, Ed., *Bufalini*, Vol. 59, Poetry. $18.

RICHARD VETERE, *Baroque*, Vol. 58, Fiction. $18.

LEWIS TURCO, *La Famiglia/The Family*, Vol. 57, Memoir, $15

NICK JAMES MILETI, *The Unscrupulous*, Vol. 56, Humanities, $20

BASSETTI, ACCOLLA, D'AQUINO, *Italici: An Encounter with Piero Bassetti*, Vol. 55, Italian Studies, $8

GIOSE RIMANELLI, *The Three-legged One*, Vol. 54, Fiction, $15

CHARLES KLOPP, *Bele Antiche Stòrie*, Vol. 53, Criticism, $25

JOSEPH RICAPITO, *Second Wave*, Vol. 52, Poetry, $12

GARY MORMINO, *Italians in Florida*, Vol. 51, History, $15

GIANFRANCO ANGELUCCI, *Federico F.*, Vol. 50, Fiction, $15

ANTHONY VALERIO, *The Little Sailor*, Vol. 49, Memoir, $9

Bordighera Press is an imprint of Bordighera, Incorporated, an independently owned not-for-profit scholarly organization that has no legal affiliation with the University of Central Florida or with The John D. Calandra Italian American Institute, Queens College/CUNY.

ROSS TALARICO, *The Reptilian Interludes*, Vol. 48, Poetry, $15

RACHEL GUIDO DE VRIES, *Teeny Tiny Tino's Fishing Story*, Vol. 47, Children's Literature, $6

EMANUEL DI PASQUALE, *Writing Anew*, Vol. 46, Poetry, $15

MARIA FAMÀ, *Looking For Cover*, Vol. 45, Poetry, $12

ANTHONY VALERIO, *Toni Cade Bambara's One Sicilian Night*, Vol. 44, Poetry, $10

EMANUEL CARNEVALI, Dennis Barone, Ed., *Furnished Rooms*, Vol. 43, Poetry, $14

BRENT ADKINS, et al., Ed., *Shifting Borders, Negotiating Places*, Vol. 42, Proceedings, $18

GEORGE GUIDA, *Low Italian*, Vol. 41, Poetry, $11

GARDAPHÈ, GIORDANO, TAMBURRI, *Introducing Italian Americana*, Vol. 40, Italian/American Studies, $10

DANIELA GIOSEFFI, *Blood Autumn/Autunno di sangue*, Vol. 39, Poetry, $15/$25

FRED MISURELLA, *Lies to Live by*, Vol. 38, Stories, $15

STEVEN BELLUSCIO, *Constructing a Bibliography*, Vol. 37, Italian Americana, $15

ANTHONY JULIAN TAMBURRI, Ed., *Italian Cultural Studies 2002*, Vol. 36, Essays, $18

BEA TUSIANI, *con amore*, Vol. 35, Memoir, $19

FLAVIA BRIZIO-SKOV, Ed., *Reconstructing Societies in the Aftermath of War*, Vol. 34, History, $30

TAMBURRI, et al., Eds., *Italian Cultural Studies 2001*, Vol. 33, Essays, $18

ELIZABETH G. MESSINA, Ed., *In Our Own Voices*, Vol. 32, Italian/American Studies, $25

STANISLAO G. PUGLIESE, *Desperate Inscriptions*, Vol. 31, History, $12

HOSTERT & TAMBURRI, Eds., *Screening Ethnicity*, Vol. 30, Italian/American Culture, $25

G. PARATI & B. LAWTON, Eds., *Italian Cultural Studies*, Vol. 29, Essays, $18

HELEN BAROLINI, *More Italian Hours*, Vol. 28, Fiction, $16

FRANCO NASI, Ed., *Intorno alla Via Emilia*, Vol. 27, Culture, $16

ARTHUR L. CLEMENTS, *The Book of Madness & Love*, Vol. 26, Poetry, $10

JOHN CASEY, et al., *Imagining Humanity*, Vol. 25, Interdisciplinary Studies, $18

ROBERT LIMA, *Sardinia/Sardegna*, Vol. 24, Poetry, $10

DANIELA GIOSEFFI, *Going On*, Vol. 23, Poetry, $10

ROSS TALARICO, *The Journey Home*, Vol. 22, Poetry, $12

EMANUEL DI PASQUALE, *The Silver Lake Love Poems*, Vol. 21, Poetry, $7

JOSEPH TUSIANI, *Ethnicity*, Vol. 20, Poetry, $12

JENNIFER LAGIER, *Second Class Citizen*, Vol. 19, Poetry, $8

FELIX STEFANILE, *The Country of Absence*, Vol. 18, Poetry, $9

PHILIP CANNISTRARO, *Blackshirts*, Vol. 17, History, $12

LUIGI RUSTICHELLI, Ed., *Seminario sul racconto*, Vol. 16, Narrative, $10

LEWIS TURCO, *Shaking the Family Tree*, Vol. 15, Memoirs, $9

LUIGI RUSTICHELLI, Ed., *Seminario sulla drammaturgia*, Vol. 14, Theater/Essays, $10

FRED GARDAPHÈ, *Moustache Pete is Dead! Long Live Moustache Pete!*, Vol. 13, Oral Literature, $10

JONE GAILLARD CORSI, *Il libretto d'autore*, 1860–1930, Vol. 12, Criticism, $17

HELEN BAROLINI, *Chiaroscuro: Essays of Identity*, Vol. 11, Essays, $15

PICARAZZI & FEINSTEIN, Eds., *An African Harlequin in Milan*, Vol. 10, Theater/Essays, $15

JOSEPH RICAPITO, *Florentine Streets & Other Poems*, Vol. 9, Poetry, $9

FRED MISURELLA, *Short Time*, Vol. 8, Novella, $7

NED CONDINI, *Quartettsatz*, Vol. 7, Poetry, $7

ANTHONY JULIAN TAMBURRI, Ed., *Fuori: Essays by Italian/American Lesbians and Gays*, Vol. 6, Essays, $10

ANTONIO GRAMSCI, P. Verdicchio, Trans. & Intro. , *The Southern Question*, Vol. 5, Social Criticism, $5

DANIELA GIOSEFFI, *Word Wounds & Water Flowers*, Vol. 4, Poetry, $8

WILEY FEINSTEIN, *Humility's Deceit: Calvino Reading Ariosto Reading Calvino*, Vol. 3,
   Criticism, $10
PAOLO A. GIORDANO, Ed., *Joseph Tusiani: Poet, Translator, Humanist*, Vol. 2, Criticism, $25
ROBERT VISCUSI, *Oration Upon the Most Recent Death of Christopher Columbus*, Vol. 1, Poetry,
   $3

CPSIA information can be obtained at www.ICGtesting.com
Printed in the USA
BVOW05s0522060614

355589BV00001B/10/P